Otte.

B51 087 447 7

KT-494-618

This book must be returned by the date specified at the time of issue as the DATE DUE FOR RETURN.

The loan may be extended (personally, by post, telephone or online) for a further period if the book is not required by another reader, by quoting the above number / author / title.

Enquiries: 01709 336774

www.rotherham.gov.uk/libraries

animal
Series editor: Jonathan Burt

Already published

Crow
Boria Sax

Ant
Charlotte Sleigh

Tortoise
Peter Young

Cockroach
Marion Copeland

Dog
Susan McHugh

Oyster
Rebecca Stott

Bear
Robert E. Bieder

Bee
Claire Preston

Rat
Jonathan Burt

Snake
Drake Stutesman

Falcon
Helen Macdonald

Whale
Joe Roman

Parrot
Paul Carter

Tiger
Susie Green

Salmon
Peter Coates

Fox
Martin Wallen

Fly
Steven Connor

Cat
Katharine M. Rogers

Peacock
Christine E. Jackson

Cow
Hannah Velten

Swan
Peter Young

Shark
Dean Crawford

Rhinoceros
Kelly Enright

Moose
Kevin Jackson

Duck
Victoria de Rijke

Horse
Elaine Walker

Elephant
Daniel Wylie

Eel
Richard Schweid

Ape
John Sorenson

Penguin
Stephen Martin

Snail
Peter Williams

Owl
Desmond Morris

Pigeon
Barbara Allen

Lion
Deirdre Jackson

Camel
Robert Irwin

Spider
Katarzyna and
Sergiusz Michalski

Otter

Daniel Allen

REAKTION BOOKS

To Anna McLaren

Published by
REAKTION BOOKS LTD
33 Great Sutton Street
London EC1V ODX, UK
www.reaktionbooks.co.uk

First published 2010
Copyright © Daniel Allen 2010

Printed and bound in China

British Library Cataloguing in Publication Data
Allen, Daniel
    Otter. – (Animal)
    1. Otters. 2. Otters – Effect of human beings on.
    I. Title II. Series
    599.7'69-DC22

    ISBN: 978 1 86189 767 1

Contents

1 Introducing the Otter

'Anyone reading through the literature on otters will be struck by how little is really known about them in the wild.'[1] This observation was made by Philip Wayre in 1977, six years after co-founding the world's first otter conservation organization. Remarkably, despite major developments in our understanding, this is still very much the case today. As Hans Kruuk noted in 2006, 'from the many studies on otters, we are left with the main message that very little is yet known about these animals.'[2] It is perhaps even more surprising that the cultural history of the otter has been totally overlooked.

As a member of the weasel family (the Mustelidae), the otter (Lutrinae) is closely related to martens, polecats, mink, skunks and badgers. Perfectly adapted for an aquatic lifestyle, fossil records suggest they derived from a common ancestor, *Mionictis*, which lived 20 million years ago. The divergence of species is thought to have taken place in the middle Miocene (see appendix, table 1). Until recent years, otter species classification was in 'a state of very considerable confusion'.[3] Clement J. Harris listed a total of 19 species and 63 sub-species in his 1968 book, *Otters: A Study of the Recent Lutrinae*. Ten years later Joseph A. Davis used new scientific evidence based on behaviour, structure and appearance.[4] He listed 9 species and 3 tribes. More recently molecular biology and DNA analysis have led to further

Eurasian otter
(*Lutra lutra*).

changes. Today scientists and conservationists generally agree there are 13 otter species with six genera.

LUTRA

1	Eurasian otter (*Lutra lutra*)
2	Hairy-nosed otter (*Lutra sumatrana*)
3	Spotted-necked otter (*Lutra maculicollis*)

LONTRA

4	Asian small-clawed otter (*Aonyx cinereus*)
5	Cape clawless otter (*Aonyx capensis*)
6	Congo clawless otter (*Aonyx congicus*)

AONYX

7	North American otter (*Lontra canadensis*)
8	Neotropical otter (*Lontra longicaudis*)
9	Southern river otter (*Lontra provocax*)
10	Marine otter (*Lontra felina*)

OTHER

11	Smooth-coated otter (*Lutrogale perspicilata*)
12	Giant otter (*Pteronura brasiliensis*)
13	Sea otter (*Enhydra lutra*)

Geographically the otter is widely distributed, found in every continent except Antarctica and Australia. Despite this, not a single species has a growing population. In 2008 all 13 appeared on the *IUCN Red List for Threatened Species*.[5] Five were categorized as endangered (2, 9, 10, 12 and 13), two as vulnerable (4, 11), and one as near threatened (1). They do share some characteristics. Every species, for instance, lives alongside or upon the water, aquatic prey is largely eaten, and of course there is the classic otter appearance: whiskered muzzle, small rounded ears, long sinuous body, thick fur, short powerful legs, large webbed feet

La Loutre, 'Front and Side View.' An original etching designed by the French artist Jacques E. de Seve, and engraved by C. Baquoy. From Buffon's *Histoire Naturelle*, c. 1760.

Colour plate of 'The Otter', engraved by Peter Mazell. From Thomas Pennant's *The British Zoology*, 1766.

and rudder-like tail. But as this chapter will show, their ecology and behaviour varies greatly. The identity of the otter is also by no means fixed or unchanging. Throughout history different people have assigned different meanings and values. Its public image has been shaped by a variety of human interactions, ranging from folkloric tales and traditional practices to commercial enterprise, sport, popular literature, television and conservation. *Otter* unravels this complicated cultural history, offering a new way of understanding the animal.

The Eurasian otter is the most widely distributed species, found in Europe, Asia and North Africa. It ranges from Ireland to Kamchatka in the north, Morocco to Indonesia in the south, and is found at sea level and in the Himalayas.[6] Inhabiting freshwater environments and rocky coastlines, they are particularly proficient swimmers, renowned for their agility and graceful movements. The naturalist Gilbert White (1837) wrote that the otter's body 'is so well formed for diving, that it makes great havoc among the inhabitants of the waters'.[7] Similarly,

Delabere Pritchett Blaine in 1840 noted their 'eel-like . . . glidings in the water actually exceed those of the finny tribes he pursues'.[8] A streamlined body and sharp instincts are assisted by sensitive whiskers which help locate prey. Their diet includes a variety of fish, eels, frogs, crayfish, crabs, birds and small mammals.

As a nocturnal and solitary animal they are rarely seen during the day, generally retiring in a sheltered hollow beside the water.[9] Typical holts range from tree roots, dried drains and stick heaps to piles of rock, thick vegetation and old burrows. Frequently on the move, the species is extremely elusive, its presence often only confirmed by visual clues left beside the water, such as the five-toed impressions of webbed feet, faeces and remains of partially eaten fish. Historically, this behaviour of leaving prey after several bites has given the animal a bad reputation.[10] Descriptions of otters living entirely on fish were once common, as was their widespread persecution (see chapter Two). In Britain, the mystery which shrouded the animal also saw it transform into a much-valued source of sport. Otter hunting was a popular pastime in the nineteenth and twentieth centuries (see chapter Four). Few people actually see the Eurasian otter in the wild, yet

An otter's streamlined body is perfectly formed for diving.

On land their movements are not as graceful. This photograph shows the ungainly run of the Eurasian otter.

it has become one of the most popular species. Henry Williamson's famous book *Tarka the Otter* (1927) helped transform the animal into a much-loved fictional character, and iconic screen star (see chapters Five and Six).

The North American otter, also known as the northern river otter, is found in fresh and coastal waters ranging from Alaska to the Gulf of Mexico, and the Pacific to Atlantic coast. Although its appearance and behaviour resembles its Eurasian relative, there are some differences. They are far more sociable. Families of three or four are common, and gregarious groups of up to 18 unrelated males have also been seen together. Male territories are also much larger, ranging up to 250 km, 170 km more than the Eurasian. Measuring up to 1.25 m, and weighing 8 to 9 kg, they are a slightly longer, more slender species. A distinctive feature is its black rhinarium, the hairless part of the nose,

Woodcut of otter
from Conrad
Gesner's *Icones
Animalium*, 1560.

which is broad and prominent. As with all otters their fur is made up of two layers: long guard hairs, which form the waterproof outer layer, and a finer, denser under-hair which provides insulation. Such pelts are highly prized by fur traders. This species is still legally killed for its fur in 29 American states and all but one Canadian province on an annual basis.[11] Their population has been maintained by regulating harvests, and monitoring numbers. Across the world other otters have not been as fortunate (see chapters Three and Seven).

Woodcut of an otter with fish, 1483.

The giant otter was once found across the Amazon Rainforest, but decades of poaching and habitat destruction have greatly reduced its distribution. Today there are fewer than 5,000 animals concentrated in the three Guyanas, and just 60 in captivity. Known locally as the river wolf, it measures up to 2 metres in length, making it the largest otter species. With its

North American otter (*Lontra canadensis*).

rounded head, bulging eyes, small outward sticking ears, large
webbed feet and flattened tail, it has a rather curious appearance. The diet of this apex predator mainly consists of fish,
such as piranhas, cichlids and catfish, although it has been
known to eat crabs, snakes and small caimans. Socially they
are gregarious, typically found in groups of up to 20 animals;
and matriarchal, led by the dominant female and her mate.

A pair of North
American otters.

The North
American otter has
a prominent black
rhinarium.

Giant otters are the largest otter species; they have long powerful bodies.

The physical appearance of the giant otter is quite unlike other otter species.

These groups are cohesive, often travelling, grooming, hunting, feeding and sleeping together. As a diurnal species they are extremely conspicuous. They mark their territory by clearing vegetation from the river bank and creating a scenting area,

OTTER MEETS LEOPARD

A Bradley model in natural Brazilian otter. Its gentle shoulders and long double-breasted line are enhanced by a sleeveless jerkin of leopard. From the new collection of original Bradley and Lanvin fur models.

The giant otter was a victim of fashion in the 1960s. They gained full protection against the commercial fur trade in 1975.

Giant otters periscoping their necks towards the photographer. Each animal has its own unique neck pattern.

known as a campsite. In this clearing 'members spend much time sprainting, urinating, depositing anal gland secretions, scraping, trampling, kneading mud, rolling, and tearing down vegetation and rubbing it over the body.'[12] By all accounts, this olfactory concoction 'stinks rather than smells'.[13] Vocal communication is also important. Nicole Duplaix identified nine distinct vocalizations including the inquisitive Hah!, explosive snorts, wavering screams, threatening growls, reassuring hums, friendly coos, whistles, squeaks and whines.

As well as being incredibly noisy, they are inquisitive. Giant otters are often seen lifting their heads out of the water 'periscoping, stretching and retracting' their necks towards unfamiliar sights and sounds, and even charging across the water towards boats.[14] Keith Laidler experienced this formidable sight when he was studying the animal in Guyana: 'They were swimming all round the canoe, red mouths ablaze, barking angrily and getting closer every second . . . this was our first view . . . I thought it might very well be our last.'[15] There are no records of giant otter attacks in the wild; however, there have been a number of fatal incidents in captivity. In 1969, for instance, a keeper fell into an enclosure at São Paulo Zoo and was killed by otters defending their cubs.[16] Similarly in 1978 an off-duty policeman was attacked at Brasilia Zoo when he saved a child who had fallen into an enclosure. The sergeant was badly bitten and later died from infections.[17]

The neotropical otter is no where near as formidable. Found throughout much of Central and South America, including the waters of the river wolf, it resembles the Eurasian otter and behaves like a North American one. It also has to contend with a number of aquatic predators such as anacondas, caiman and piranhas. Although the species is thought to be widespread, scientists are 'rather ignorant of its biology';[18] its population is also unknown. The IUCN found there was inadequate information to make an assessment of its risk of extinction in 2008. It therefore appears as 'data deficient' on the *IUCN Red List of Threatened Species*.

The southern river otter or huillin has also 'had little scientific attention,' despite having the 'smallest geographical range of all otters'.[19] This is due to its solitary, nocturnal behaviour and isolated habitat. Within the Patagonian region of Chile and Argentina, this endangered species is clinging on for survival,

Giant otters are extremely protective of their cubs.

found in just seven areas from Cautin to Futaleufú. The marine otter, known locally as the sea cat, is in a similar predicament. One of the smaller otter species, it has adapted to a saltwater environment. It has coarse, rough fur and feeds on crabs, fish and molluscs. It once flourished along the Pacific coast from Peru to the southern tip of Argentina.[20] Today the species is on the brink of extinction with less than 1,000 animals left in the wild, and none in captivity.

Three species are endemic to Asia. The smooth-coated otter is more robust than its Eurasian counterpart, and as its name suggests has shorter (12–14 mm guard hair, 6–8 mm under-hair), smoother fur. Distributed throughout the Indian subcontinent and Southeast Asia, these conspicuous animals live in small groups, usually five strong. When Gavin Maxwell wrote *Ring of Bright Water* in 1960, this species rose to fame. Mijbil, the otter found in the Iraqi marshes and taken back to Scotland, was in fact an unknown sub-species. Much to the surprise of Wilfred Thesiger, who actually found the animal, it was named after the author, *Lutrogale perspicillata maxwelli*. Sadly Maxwell's otter is now regarded as extinct (see chapters Five and Six).[21]

The hairy-nosed otter is the rarest of all the otter species. Similar in appearance to the Eurasian, it is distinguished by the hairs which grow on its rhinarium, hence its rather charming name. Once found in the open swamps and reed meadows of Southeast Asia, it was thought to be extinct in 1998. Fortunately it was rediscovered in Vietnam the following year, and has since been found in Thailand, Sumatra and Cambodia. As this otter is said to be the 'most difficult to identify in the field',[22] very little is actually known about the species. With an estimated population of fewer than 300 it is now considered one of the most endangered species in the world. The survival of *Lutra sumatrana* recently experienced another setback. In June 2008 an animal rescued from a Cambodian fisherman became the world's only captive hairy-nosed otter. Dara, as he was known, resided in a specially built enclosure at Phnom Tamau Zoological Garden and Rescue Centre, near Phnom Penh. Annette Olsson, a research manager for Conservation International, initially had high hopes: 'Scientists recommend establishment of a breeding population in captivity to ensure survival of this species. Dara could be the founder of such a captive population, if and when we find him a wife, of course.'[23] Sadly a mate was not found, and Dara died of a lung infection in spring 2010. The post mortem also revealed stomach ulcers.

A species which has benefited from captive breeding is the Asian small-clawed otter (also known as the Oriental small-clawed otter). The smallest otter species, they are known for their gregarious behaviour, distinctive finger-like front claws, and being the least proficient swimmers of all otters. Their natural habitat in southern India and Southeast Asia ranges from freshwater swamp forests to rice fields, mangroves, streams and reservoirs. Most people, however, will be familiar with their

Dara, the world's only hairy-nosed otter, died in spring 2010. He is now recognized as an ambassador for otter conservation.

appearance as their playful antics and excitable chirps are seen and heard in zoos across the world. They breed particularly well in captivity, having as many as seven cubs in a litter, and are relatively tame. In the 1970s a hand-reared small-clawed otter called Mouse 'personified the Otter Trust', even though the organization was primarily concerned with the British *Lutra lutra*. Philip Wayre, co-founder of the Trust, reflected: 'it is probably true to say that through his close contact with such a large number of people Mouse contributed more to the conservation of otters by arousing public interest and concern than any human being has done.'[24] The species is still raising public awareness in the twenty-first century. In 2007 there were 666 captive animals on public display, far more than any other otter species.[25]

The other two members of the *Aonyx* genus are found in Africa. Both the Cape clawless and Congo clawless (also known as the swamp otter) are much larger than the small-clawed, measuring up to 1.5 m and 1.8 m respectively. They use their dextrous forefeet to catch prey, including slow-moving fish, crabs, molluscs, insects and frogs. The Cape clawless is distributed throughout

The Asian small-clawed otter is the smallest otter species. These sociable animals live in extended family groups.

Asian small-clawed otters are a popular attraction in zoos across the world.

The co-founder and 'personification' of the Otter Trust, Philip Wayre, and Mouse.

Aonyx cinerea have distinctive partially webbed forefeet.

much of sub-Saharan Africa, from Senegal and Kenya to South Africa,[26] whereas the swamp otter is only found in the Congo basin. Owing to difficulties in the region a 'detailed ecological study' has yet to be conducted on this species.[27] The clawless otters share their habitat with the spotted-necked otter (sometimes classified as *Hydrictis maculicollis*). The species is abundant in central Africa, particularly Lake Victoria and Lake Tanganyika, but notably absent in far western and southern Africa. As a member of the *Lutra* genera they are equipped with webbed feet, a broad fleshy muzzle, and teeth adapted for catching fish. They are also amongst the best swimmers. In Swahili they are known as the water hyena (fisi maji); the irregular mottled patches of white that appears on their chest and legs account for its names.

The sea otter is strikingly different. Residing in the shallow coastal waters of the northern Pacific Ocean, its three subspecies are found in Russian (*Enhydra l. lutris*), Alaskan (*E. l. kenyoni*) and Californian (*E. l. nereis*) waters. The characteristic habitat is over a kelp forest no more than 1 km from the shore. Their appearance and behaviour are quite unique. As well as being the heaviest otter, it is the largest member of the weasel family, and only marine mammal. They generally 'eat, sleep, mate and are born and raised in water',[28] and spend most of their lives floating belly-up on the surface. On the rare occasions that they do venture ashore their movement is by no means graceful.

At sea the species survives rough and freezing conditions. Where most marine mammals are kept warm by an insulating layer of fat, the sea otter is protected by an extremely dense layer of fur. Ranging from 26,000 to 165,000 hairs per square centimetre, it is the densest coat in the animal kingdom. This fact did not go unnoticed by international fur traders, who hunted the species to the brink of extinction in the nineteenth century (see chapter Three).

Sea otters maintain their body warmth in two ways. First, they take a lot of time grooming their coat. The air which is pressed from their fur during dives is not naturally restored. The animal lifts fur to its mouth, and painstakingly blows air into it, restoring insulation.[29] Second, they have a very high metabolism, eating 30 per cent of their body weight in a day. This is two and a half times more than a terrestrial mammal, giving them one of the biggest appetites of all mammals in proportion to their size.[30] Although their diet varies it mostly consists of sea urchins, crabs, abalones, clams, squid and slow-moving fish. This diet makes them an important keystone predator. Grazing sea urchins have the capacity to wipe out underwater kelp forests. By controlling their abundance, sea otters enhance kelp

clockwise from top left:
The fur of the sea otter is the densest in the animal kingdom.

Sea otter with sea urchin.

A raft of sea otters.

A sea otter wrapped in kelp secures its position above the kelp forest.

forest ecosystems, enlarge fish stocks, and attract fish-eating birds and mammals.[31]

During the forage for food their flipper-like hind feet propel them to depths of up to 100 metres. Their front paws are much shorter, with tough pads and retractable claws. These are used for gripping prey from the seabed. The sea otter is well known for being one of the few tool-using mammals. Its habit of using a stone as an anvil to break open hard-shelled molluscs has been well documented. While floating on its back a stone is rested on the chest, and a shell is held tightly between the paws. The mollusc is then struck against the stone until the shell breaks and its contents can be devoured.[32] To prevent drifting away with the current they often drape their bodies with kelp. Their social organization is also distinctive. Although sea otters are usually alone, these gregarious animals aggregate in huge groups known as rafts; the largest reported contained 2,000 animals. Males and females are also strongly segregated. A fine example of this can be found on the Californian coast between Los Angeles and San Francisco. A group of males is found at each end of the 150 km stretch, with a female group in the middle.[33] Groups of animals floating on the open seas made the species particularly vulnerable to human persecution.

2 Folklore, Fables, Tradition and the Otter

Although scientific understanding is now given priority over myth, the meanings and values of animals were once derived from folkloric tales, fables and traditional practices. The relationship between people and the otter has developed over the centuries. Across the world attitudes towards the animal have been shaped by different symbolic, moral, mythical and practical interpretations, many of which have been long forgotten. Some of the portrayals may now raise an eyebrow, or even a smile, but they are significant parts of the animal's cultural history.

The otter features in several religions. In ancient Persia the animal was valued above all others. The Zoroastrian people believed it was against nature and their god to kill the otter, and would hold ceremonies for those they found dead in the wild. The animal was so sacred that the Zoroastrian scriptures (in the *Avesta: Vendidad*) detailed 18 severe penalties for 'the murder of a water-dog', including the perpetrator being made to kill 10,000 frogs, 10,000 snakes, 10,000 worms and 10,000 corpse-flies. He would also be forced to carry 10,000 loads of cleansed wood to the sacred fire, and give away land, property, all his wealth and even his daughter to 'godly men'.[1]

Animals also had a moral and symbolic role in the Christian faith, as demonstrated by the *Physiologus*. Written by an unknown Greek philosopher roughly in the fourth century, its

The Hydrus, depicted as an otter, eats its way out of the crocodile's side having crawled into its mouth, c. 1200.

lud animalest mmlo flunto q̄o dicmir' hydrus. pbisiologus dicr̄ deo qnoo senss est hoc animal munici cocodrillo. ꝗ hanc habet naturam ꝫ con sueudmem. ꝗum uider cocodrillum in lrroribus fluminis ꝟommienrem apꝭ oꝛt uadir ꝫ muolmr se in lunum lur q̄o

chapters told tales of beasts, birds and nature to teach Christian dogma. The hydrus is a notable example. Over the centuries it has been depicted as a water-snake, dragon, bird and otter. The last has become more widely associated with the allegory in recent years, as the following passage from 1896 proves: 'When the crocodile sleeps, it keeps its mouth open; but the otter wallows in the mire until it becomes thickly coated with mud, which dries and hardens and forms a sort of armor, thus enabling it to run securely into the jaws and down the throat of the sleeping crocodile, and to kill it by devouring its bowels.'[2] This signifies the Lord's (otter's) descent into hell (the crocodile), his victory over Satan, and rising from the grave.

Many of the early Christian stories about saints also featured wild animals. The mythologized relationship between saints and the natural world evoked closeness with God. The otter is associated with two patron saints. The first is St Kevin (AD 498–618)

Two otters warm the feet of St Cuthbert, a modern icon by Aidan Hart.

ST.
CU
TH
BE
RT

of Glendalough, County Wicklow. According to legend, one winter night he waded into a lake, recited his prayers, and accidentally dropped his breviary. As it disappeared into the icy water he feared it would never be seen again. Only moments later an otter swam to the surface with the undamaged book in its mouth, and returned it to the monk. This same otter appeared in later times of need. When there was danger of starvation at the monastery the animal brought salmon every day. The otter, however, sensed that one of the monks had imagined his pelt as a pair of gloves and never returned again. With this, the altruism and generosity of the otter was set against the selfish and greedy thoughts of the monk.[3]

The second famous legend, of St Cuthbert (*c.* AD 634–687) and the otters, comes from England. This Northumbrian monk used to discreetly slip out of his monastery at night, much to the intrigue of his fellow order members. One night a monk quietly followed him outside the monastery walls, and the sight he witnessed was quite remarkable. Cuthbert walked into the sea, waded up to his neck, raised his arms to the sky and prayed. When he came to shore, he was not alone: 'There followed in his footsteps two little sea animals, humbly prostrating themselves on the

In southern Sweden petroglyphs dating back to 1000 BC were found in Kivik, featuring stylized animals which appear to represent captive otters.

earth; and, licking his feet, they rolled upon them, wiping them with their skins and warming them with their breath.'[4] These otters continued offering their warmth until a blessing had been received. The next time the monk met Cuthbert he fell to his feet, confessed to following him, wept and begged for his forgiveness. The monk was readily forgiven and, on being asked, happily agreed not to mention the miracle again in Cuthbert's lifetime.

In France the Carthusian monks had a very different relationship with the animal. Forbidden to eat meat, they classified the otter as a fish and duly ate it. When Thomas Pennant observed this in the mid-eighteenth century, he wrote: 'Its flesh is excessively rank and fishy. The Romish church permits the use of [the otter] on maigre days. In the kitchen, of the . . . convent near Dijon, we saw one preparing for the dinner of the religious of that rigid order who, by their rules, are prohibited during their whole lives to eat flesh.'[5]

For the Ainu, an aboriginal people from the northernmost islands of Japan, the otter had an important role in the story of creation. According to folklore, the god of heaven sent a sparrow to the god of creation to tell him that man should be made from wood, not stone. When the god of heaven changed his mind the duty of messenger was passed to the otter. On seeing a pool of glistening water the animal soon became distracted with swimming and playing, and totally forgot about the message. The consequence was that man, in being made out of wood rather than stone, remained mortal. The otter was punished in various ways for this. In one interpretation, 'the god of heaven became angry and trod upon the face of the otter', which 'explains why the otter has such an ugly face'.[6] In another the animal was given such a bad memory that if a person were to eat an otter's head, they would become as forgetful as the creature. Those who did happen to desire such a feast could

'Who Killed Otter's
Babies', illustration
from Walter Skeat's
*Fables and Folk
Tales from an
Eastern Forest*,
1901.

take precautions to avoid ill-fortune. As Reverend John
Batchelor wrote in *The Ainu and their Folklore* (1901): 'When eating it the people must take their swords, knives, axes, bows and
arrows, tobacco boxes and pipes, trays, cups . . . and everything
they possess, tie them up in bundles with carrying slings, and sit
with them attached to their heads while in the act of eating . . .
If this method be carefully adhered to, there will be no danger
of forgetting where a thing has been placed, otherwise loss of
memory will be the result.'[7]

In Southeast Asia the otter has appeared in many fables. 'Who Killed Otter's Babies' is a wonderful moral tale. The following version is based on the story as told by Walter Skeat in *Fables and Folk Tales from an Eastern Forest* (1901):

Mouse-deer was looking after Otter's babies one day while Otter went out to catch fish. When he returned he was horrified to find his babies dead and crushed flat. 'I'm very sorry,' said Mouse-deer 'but I'm the War-Dancer and Woodpecker sounded the war-gong. I had to dance and accidentally trod on your children.'

Otter was furious and ran to King Solomon to seek justice for his family. Mouse-deer was hauled up before the king's court, and admitted 'I accidentally killed Otter's babies while dancing to the sound of Woodpecker's war-gong.'

King Solomon asked Woodpecker why the gong had been sounded.

He said, 'I'm the Chief-Beater and I hit the war-gong because I saw Great Lizard armed with his sword.'

Great Lizard explained, 'I wore my sword because I saw Tortoise wearing his coat of mail.'

Tortoise stepped forward, 'I wore my armor because I saw Crab aiming his trident.'

Crab insisted, 'I aimed my trident because I saw Crayfish brandishing his spear.'

Crayfish maintained, 'I brandished my spear because I saw Otter coming down the river to kill my children!'

And with this King Solomon made his judgement, 'If that is the case, the Otter himself killed the Otter's children, and the Mouse-deer cannot be blamed, by the law of the land!'[8]

In this sequence of events the otter is used to show how the action of one person always impacts upon the lives of others. The tale teaches its listeners to be aware of themselves, and to always take responsibility for their behaviour.

In Native American tradition the otter was feared by some nations, but highly revered by others. Along the Pacific Northwest Coast the Haida, Heiltsuk, Tlingit and Tsimshian were fearful of land otters. Dwelling primarily in the roots of trees, these animals became known as root people, or Kuschtas. The Kuschtas were cunning tricksters who could transform into human form at will. They were feared as they freely capsized

A Tlingit shaman's wooden mask of a man in the process of transforming into a land otter.

boats and kidnapped near-drowned people. In Tlingit myths unwary travellers were also visited by deceased relatives or seemingly friendly guests. When they ate the feast which had been prepared for them they were put under a spell and slowly lost all human characteristics. It was said that only a shaman's intervention would save these kidnapped souls from a life amongst the roots.[9] The otter became a totem of shamans because of these supernatural powers to charm and transform.[10]

The animal was also valued for its perceived healing powers. The Midewin people, or Grand Medicine society, of the Great Lakes Region greatly esteemed it as a sacred spirit. According to

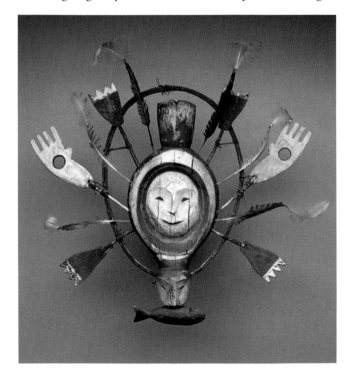

Eskimo mask in the form of an otter.

their creation myth, the Midewin came into existence after the servant (Great Rabbit) of the Good Spirit saw the helpless condition of the original people. Great Rabbit, who wanted them to have the means to overcome starvation and disease, chose to communicate with the people through an otter. He shared the mysteries and secrets of the Midewin with the animal, and handed him the sacred drum, rattle, and tobacco for curing the sick. Using his medicine bag he then 'shot' a sacred white shell, the *mi'gis*, into the body of the otter, giving him immortality and the ability to pass on these secrets to the original people. This myth accounts for the widespread use of otter-skin medicine bags and their central role in healing ceremonies. The ritual involving the *mi'gis* was replicated in an elaborate ceremony which ended with a patient spitting the shell from their mouth, a sign that their bodies had been entered by supernatural power.[11]

Amongst the Iroquois League, the Mohawk, Oneida, Onondaga, Cayuga, Seneca and Tuscararo nations, there was a group called the Otter Society. Its membership consisted solely of women who taught people 'how to give thanks to the water animals, to retain their favour, and to cure illnesses brought on by transgressions against the water animals'.[12] Their rituals did not involve singing, dancing or the use of shells; instead they were said to cure by sprinkling sacred healing water over patients. The Crow Nation of Montana, on the other hand, had a much more elaborate ritual. Chief Plenty Coups gave a detailed description of this in his 1930 biography. He wrote:

> The-fringe wound a strip of otter skin around his head, tossed another strip, which had been cut so as to include the animal's tail, over his shoulder, and, singing to the drums of his helpers, lifted his medicine out if its bundle. It was a whole otter's skin, with the head stuffed . . . He

whistled like an otter, dipped the medicine skin in a paunch kettle of water, and sprinkled it upon the wounded man, while the helpers sang to their drums. The young man sat up . . . They walked into the river, where The-fringe dived like an otter, smoothly, and without disturbing the water . . . the otter skin seemed itself to be alive and swimming. Then I saw its nose at the wounds of the young man, saw its tail wiggle in the water as if it sucked blood and was pleased . . . Red blood came quickly, and as quickly The-fringe stopped it. 'You are healed,' I heard him say. And this was true. The young man was well again. Two lumpy scars were where the holes had been.[13]

Alongside these folkloric portrayals, the otter has gained a universal reputation as a fish-killer. A consequence of this has been centuries of worldwide persecution. In England, and later Britain, the monarchy played a leading role in the organized killing of otters. Kings and queens from the Plantagenet dynasty

'The Otter', from *The Master of Game*, c. 1410.

37

through to the Hanoverians employed an otter hunter (King's Otterer) and maintained a pack of otterhounds (otter dogges) to protect the valuable fish stocks of inland fisheries. The first recorded pack was established in 1157. Under the royal patronage of King Henry II, Roger Follo was appointed the King's Otterer.[14] This position came with a large manor, known as Otterer's Fee, in Aylesbury, Buckinghamshire. In 1422 Henry VI appointed William Melbourne as Valet of our Otter-Hounds. Melbourne's huntsman was paid tuppence a day to hunt with eight hounds.

The animal was seen as even more of a problem in the sixteenth century. In 1557 Queen Mary ordered the Norwich Assembly to insist that freshwater fishermen on the River Yare 'keep a dog to hunt the otter, and to make a general hunt twice or

Otter hunt in 15th-century France. From Gaston Phoebus' *Book of the Hunt.*

Hunting scenes in the Netherlands, c. 1578.

thrice in the year or more, at time or times convenient, upon pain to forfeit ten shillings'.[15] In 1566 the Acte for the Preservation of Grayne was passed. This was significant since the otter, along with seven other animals, was reclassified as vermin. Under this legislature parish constables and churchwardens were given new powers to offer bounties for the heads of badgers, foxes, hedgehogs, otters, polecats, stoats, weasels and wildcats. Bounty prices reflected the perceived 'pest value' of vermin in any given parish. In Doncaster in 1619, for example, a dead otter attracted six pence, compared to four pence for a polecat, and two pence for a weasel.[16] With this law the practice of killing was duly encouraged.

The animal was targeted by all manner of people. Otter hunters were initially seen as experts in pest control, and otter killing provided a small income. By the 1770s there was widespread opposition to the animal: 'What miles Whitaker has traversed in pursuit of this fish destroyer! The banks of the Torne, Trent and Don were trodden again and again by his unwearied

feet . . . Every hall and mansion of consequence in the neighbourhood received him . . . the more he protected the "Stew ponds", the more cordial were his receptions.'[17] Though otter-hunting did not become widely accepted as a source of sport until the nineteenth century, the animal was described in terms that emphasized its role as an invader and devourer of fish, such as fish monger, fish slicer, varmint, cunning marauder and four-legged fisher. Wildlife painters and natural history illustrators reinforced this reputation, invariably depicting the animal alongside dead fish.

The otter was particularly disliked by the angling community, who turned to lutracide. Isaak Walton had, of course, set out a clear contract with the animal in *The Compleat Angler* (1653):

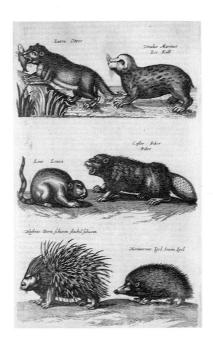

Joannes Jonstonus, Otter, Beaver and Porcupines, engraving from *Historiae naturalis de quadrupedibus*, 1657.

'I am, Sir, a Brother of the Angle, and therefore an enemy of the Otter; for I hate them perfectly, because they love fish so well.'[18] As the readership grew, the opinion of Walton became more deeply instilled in the angling fraternity.[19] By the twentieth century the soaring popularity of angling meant that well-stocked stretches of river were in demand.[20] Riparian owners killed otters as their presence devalued their waters. For the more affluent game angler or angling association the inflated price of water rights meant that rented stretches of water were expensive purchases. The desire to safeguard such investments heightened inclinations to kill. For coarse anglers who spent relatively little, on the other hand, preventing the otter from killing future possible catches was a good enough excuse.

Remarkably, the fish-catching skills of the otter were not condemned by everyone. Across the world small pockets of fishermen appreciated this talent and trained the animal to assist them. Fishing with otters can be traced back to south-west China in the sixth century. During the Tang Dynasty the practice was prevalent in Szechwan; centuries later it was observed by Europeans on the Yangtze River. In the 1320s Friar Odoric wrote: 'They fish by means of another fish called a diver. They keep it by a cord attached to a fine collar. It has a muzzle and neck like a fox, forepaws like a dog, hind feet like a duck and the body of a fish. It dives into the water and I swear in less than two hours it had filled two big baskets, always depositing

John James Audubon, *Otter Caught in a Trap*, oil on canvas, 1826.

Otter fishing in Bangladesh.

the fish in the baskets.'[21] Another method involved the otter
being released into the water and herding fish into nets.[22] Since
the fifteenth century these practices have also been used in
Burma, Malaysia, Sumatra, Thailand, northern Africa, Scan-
dinavia, Poland, Germany, England and Scotland. Eurasian and
smooth coated otters were the favoured species. William Bingley,
the nineteenth century naturalist, recognized the difficulties of

'Otter', coloured plate from *The Natural History of Quadrupeds and Cetaceous Animals*, 1811.

training but insisted it was worthwhile: 'The training of them . . . requires both assiduity and perseverance: but their activity and use, when taught, sufficiently repay this trouble; and few animals are more beneficial to their masters.'[23] Individuals from Bangladesh and India are still reaping the rewards from such perseverance today.

This tradition is now largely overshadowed by historical practices of otter persecution. Commercial killing for fur took its toll on otter populations, and the practice of hunting for sport, or indeed killing for fun, brought the animal to a new literary audience. Folkloric tales have also led to indiscriminate killing, albeit to a lesser extent. In Indonesia, for instance, there is a story that otters have a magical stone in their body which allows them to swim well underwater. It is said that these qualities are transferred to any individual who has the stone in their possession. This has contributed to the plight of the hairy-nosed otter.[24] Body parts have also been valued for their supposed medicinal properties. Centuries ago in the Scottish Highlands, the dried and powdered skin was used to treat smallpox and fevers. Similarly it was thought that a person could gain the

Ulisse Aldrovandi, *Lutra*, woodcut.

power to cure burns simply by licking the liver of a freshly killed otter.[25] The traditional remedy for fevers in the Aleutian Islands was powdered otter penis bone,[26] in India powdered otter testicles were said to improve sexual potency,[27] and in Kenya dried pieces of otter meat crushed and mixed with body oils were used 'as an ointment charm to attract the lover's heart'.[28] Although these medicines sound rather bizarre today the Asian and African examples are in fact still prevalent in the twenty-first century.

3 Commercial Otter Hunting

As with all fur-bearing animals otters have endured centuries of persecution from the fur trade. One of the earliest historical records of their commercial value dates back to 1408 in Ireland, when a 'lowly serf' was charged a penalty of 164 otter skins for arrears of rent by King Henry IV.[1] Across the world otters have continued to be killed for tradition, fashion and profit, so much so that many species are now on the brink of extinction. The one species which has suffered more than any other at the hands of commercial hunting is the sea otter. Today this animal is widely labelled as both a victim and a survivor, yet its economic and political past has been largely forgotten. The history of the sea otter is entangled with the expansion of Russian imperialism, the suffering of indigenous peoples, the commercial opening of the Pacific Ocean, and the shaping of American frontier history.

The fur of the sea otter was once considered the most valuable in the world. It was exceptionally dense, as has already been mentioned, ranging from 26,000 to 165,000 hairs per square centimetre, and became a highly sought-after fashion item amongst the wealthy. Although indigenous peoples had killed the animal for its fur and flesh for thousands of years, commercial hunting only started in the mid-eighteenth century. This international trade had a rather unexpected beginning. In 1741

Vitus Bering set off on an expedition to map the west coast of Alaska. When the storm-ravaged ship ran ashore and the captain died, the remaining crew made shelters and survived by eating sea cows (which became extinct just 28 years later), seals and sea otters. They found the sea otter particularly easy to kill. 'The beasts had never seen man before and had no reason to fear them', explains Roy Nickerson. 'They went up to the haggard Russians like a group of kittens seeking lunch. As they rubbed their noses joyously against the legs of the hungry sailors, they were bludgeoned to death, then skinned and eaten.'[2] Amongst

During rough storms sea otters ventured to land. This made them vulnerable to clubbing from indigenous peoples and commercial hunters.

Sea otter swimming on its back (top), and walking on land (bottom). Illustration by Georg Wilhelm Steller, 1751.

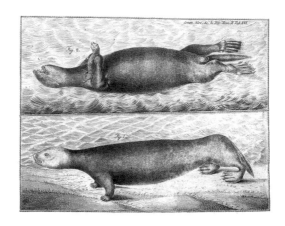

the bored men gambling was prevalent, and these skins became the main prize. The qualities of this fur did not go unnoticed by Georg Steller, the appointed naturalist of the expedition. He wrote: 'These animals are very beautiful, and because of their beauty are very valuable, as one may well believe of a skin the hairs of which, an inch or an inch and a half in length, are very soft, very thickly set, jet black and glossy.'[3] Another noted feature was that the fur was always in its prime, and therefore the otter could be hunted all year round.

When the 46 surviving members constructed a new vessel in 1742 they eventually returned to Russia with nearly 700 pelts. Steller credited the sea otter for their survival, insisting the animal deserved 'great reverence' for preventing scurvy and starvation.[4] The arrival of these new skins caused quite a sensation, especially in China, where the Manchu upper classes initially paid up to $100 per pelt. As these high prices were unrivalled in the trade, the sea otter soon became known as 'soft gold'. When explorers and traders learnt that sea otters were essentially floating fortunes, there was a frenzied rush to the northwest

Floating belly up on the water, rafts of sea otters were easy targets for commercial hunters.

Pacific coast. The Russians were the first to organize large-scale commercial hunting expeditions. The fur hunter entrepreneurs, known as *promyshlenniks*, quickly moved in: 'one hundred ventures obtained more than 8,000,000 silver roubles' from 1743 to 1800.[5] During this time settlements were established and otter populations plundered in the Kurilian-Kamchatkan Islands, the Aleutian Islands and the Northwest Coast. 'Time after time, as new colonies of sea otters were found, the hunters would move in and reduce the population to a vestige or to extinction, often over a very short time indeed.'[6]

Of the competing fur trading companies, the Golikov-Shelikhov Company was one of the most powerful. Their search for the sea otter led Grigory Shelikhov to establish the first permanent Russian settlement in Alaska in 1784. Three Saints Bay on Kodiak Island became an important base for further exploration and hunting expeditions. Another influential figure, Alexandr Baranov, was hired to manage this fur enterprise from 1790. His involvement reveals the scale and pace of the organized killing. In January 1795, for instance, he sailed to Sitka Sound, placed a cross in the uninhabited shore, and named the waters Cross Bay. Eighteen months later a party of Kodiak Aleut hunters was sent there and 1,847 sea otters were killed. In the summer of 1798 another 1,000 were bagged. The following year he returned to Cross Bay with 550 kayaks of Aleut hunters, and established a new settlement, Archangel.[7] The tsarist government also took monopolistic control over the fur trade in 1799, imposing a 10 per cent tax on the value of all shipments. All previous ventures were united as the Russian-American Company (RAC), and Baranov was appointed first governor. Archangel, today known as Sitka, became the head-quarters. Under this new leadership, hunting districts were established to help maintain otter populations. A system was adopted where each district was hunted for two years then rested for three.[8] The RAC extended their hunting grounds further down the west coast of North America, in 1812, when they established a settlement at Fort Ross, California. At this time the Californian sea otter population was between 16,000 and 20,000.

Sea otter hunting did not only involve the exploitation of animals; indigenous communities also suffered. Harold Mc-Cracken made this point in *Hunters of the Stormy Sea:* 'The story of the sea-otter hunters and the hundred-year rule of the Russians on the North-west Coast of America is a saga of one primitive man's most rigorous conquests of nature, combined with one of the most ruthless eras of human subjugation, cruelty, and rapine in frontier history.'[9] Hunting at sea did not come naturally to the Russians, but colonial rule did. When they realized that the Aleuts were expert hunters the Russians forced them to work for them. They did this by taking women and children prisoner and forcing the men to hunt. If a hunter made a poor showing, he was tortured or, occasionally, shot.[10] By the nineteenth century the 'Aleutian chain was like a trail of blood';[11] 150,000 sea otters had been killed and the Aleut population had been reduced from 20,000 to 2,000.

The Aleuts captured sea otters on a regular basis as they not only had traditional knowledge of the animal and its environment, but also owned the best equipment and used the most productive methods. This meant, as the following eyewitness account proves, that they appeared to be naturals on the water:

> The Aleutians dressed in their water-proof garments, made from the intestines of seals, wedge themselves into their baidarkas (which are constructed with a light, wooden frame, and covered with walrus or seal skin) and, donning their hunting caps, plunge through the surf that dashes high along the crags, and with almost instinctive skill, reach the less turbulent ground-swell that heaves in every direction. These aquatic men are so closely confined by the narrow build of their boats, and keeping in motion with them, too, that their appearance suggests the idea that some undescribed marine monster just emerged from the depths below.[12]

Once at sea, four methods were available for killing: the use of nets, clubbing, surf-shooting, and spearing surround. The Aleuts specialized in the last. For this, a party of up to twenty baidarkas, each containing two men, would paddle to an area that otters were known to frequent. They would then spread out in a line and quietly search. Once an otter had been sighted the hunter would raise his paddle as a signal, dash towards it and throw his spear. If the otter dived beneath the water, the hunter would position his kayak directly above the point of disappearance. By this stage, it had little chance of escaping. The kayaks

This hunting scene in Alaska shows a circle of baidarkas waiting for the sea otter to rise to the surface. Drawing by H. W. Elliott.

would scatter and form a half-mile wide circle, then patiently wait. When the otter reappeared for breath the nearest hunter would dart towards the animal. On this occasion, however, the aim was to startle it. As Alexander Allan wrote in *Hunting the Sea Otter* (1910): 'all hands shout and throw their spears to make the animal dive again as quickly as possible, thus giving it scarcely an instant to recover itself.'[13] This routine would be repeated until it became an easy target on the surface of the water. As this could take up to three hours, perseverance was crucial.

The Aleuts were such efficient killers that the Russians were dependent on them. RAC officials even acknowledged this in an 1861 report: 'in chatting with the Aleuts, and in fact with all the natives, we have come to the conclusion that they are not in slavery to the Company at all, but that in fact the Company itself has become a slave to them.'[14]

The sea otter effectively belonged to the Russians until the 1780s, as they kept the commercial value of the animal a closely guarded secret. When other countries realized just how much money could be made hundreds of ships were sent from Britain, Spain, France and America. The British stumbled upon

Chief at Nootka Sound with an arrow case made of sea otter skin, 1778.

the lucrative trade quite by accident during Captain James Cook's last voyage (1776–80). While trading in the Pacific many items were obtained, including sea otter skins. They were appreciated for their warmth but not highly valued. Some crewmen even used them as blankets and mattresses. When HMS

Discovery and HMS *Resolution* arrived at a trading post in Macao, the skins were the source of much excitement for the Chinese merchants. Great sums of money were exchanged, with well-preserved skins fetching £40 each. The following extract from Cook's journal reveals just how surprised the explorers were by the discovery:

> The whole amount of value, on both ships, I am confident did not fall short of two thousand pounds sterling . . . and at least two-thirds of the quantity we had originally got from the Americans were spoiled or even worn out, or had been given away . . . The advantages that might be derived from a voyage to that part of the American coast, undertaken with commercial view, appears to me of a degree of importance to call for the attention of the Public.[15]

These advantages became public knowledge in 1784 when Cook's *Voyage of the Pacific Ocean* was published. The promise of instant wealth inspired many international merchants, who

This engraving of a sea otter appears in the published account of Captain James Cook's final voyage.

went to great lengths to obtain it. One contemporary Spanish observer noted: 'the English, and more especially the Americans, give anything they have, or for which the natives may beg, in exchange for the skins of the sea otter.'[16]

The plight of the sea otter intensified as its fur reached the heights of fashion in St Petersburg, Paris, London and Boston. At Canton, the international hub for the maritime fur trade, the relative value of pelts is rather instructive. In 1810–11, for instance, a sea otter pelt was worth $21.50, compared to $6.50 for a beaver, and only $2 for the much larger fur seal.[17] The figures mentioned are staggering. From 1790 to 1818 279,455 sea otter skins were shipped to Canton, almost 10,000 annually for three decades; 158,070 were sold by American traders alone in 1804–37. And an estimated 750,000 or more skins were sold by everyone involved between 1745 and 1822.[18] This had a devastating impact on the sea otter population. The Russians, who were fully aware of this, implemented a range of conservation measures. In 1828 the people of Sanak Island, a sea otter stronghold, were relocated to the Alaska Peninsula. Also in their hunting grounds, annual caps for killing were introduced, hunting grounds were rotated, females and pups became protected, individuals were prevented from buying pelts from the Aleuts, and new settlements close to sea otter hauling grounds were prohibited.[19] By the 1830s the annual cull from Alaska had dropped to 1,000–2,000.

This restraint meant there were still enough otters left to make hunting worthwhile in the late 1860s. In 1867 the United States purchased Alaska from the Russian Empire for $7,200,000. An American firm also bought the rights to the Russian-American Company this year, renaming it the Alaska Commercial Company. This territorial transfer attracted many individual sea otter hunters to the region. The previous conservation measures were not continued under American rule, instead the exploitation intensified. This generation of hunters preferred to use guns and nets. When new laws were introduced they were flouted. Lydia Black notes: 'When the government reserved the right of taking sea otters to the Natives, many of these hunters married Native women. By 1886 Aleuts appealed to President Cleveland protesting the practice and also protesting the taking of sea otters with breech-loading rifles.'[20] Over the next forty years fur traders reaped the rewards, with skin sales far exceeding the

A gentleman proudly stands beside three sea otter skins in 1892.

price paid for the Alaskan territory.[21] It was, however, a very different story for the sea otter.

The unregulated exploitation was exterminating the species. Colonies had already disappeared from former strongholds, and the animal was increasingly difficult to find. The first American authority to criticize this was Henry W. Elliott, a special agent investigating US government interests in Alaska. In 1874 he reported that sea otter stocks were being mismanaged and that legal protection was required:

Skins of an adult and young sea otter are displayed together in Unalaska, 1892.

Now, during the last season, instead of less than seven hundred skins as obtained by the Russians, our trade has secured not much less than four thousand. This immense difference is not due to the fact of there being a proportionate increase of sea otters, but to organisation. Yet the keen competition of our traders will ruin the business in a comparatively short time if some action is not taken by the Government.[22]

This recommendation was not acted upon. Elliott published his book on Alaska, *Our Arctic Province*, in 1886. He seemed fascinated by the history of sea otter hunting, but frustrated at just how oblivious those who indirectly funded the practice were:

Little does my lady think, as she contemplates the rich shimmer of the ebony sea-otter trimming to her new seal-skin sacque, that the quest of the former has engaged thousands of men during the last century in exhaustive deeds of hazardous peril . . . venturesome labor and

The lady on the left is wrapped in a cloak with sea otter fur trimming. Such garments were fashionable in the early nineteenth century.

Sea otter fur was still sought after in 1900. This cutting from the Furs World Fair in Paris shows a gentleman modelling a coat with sea otter fur trimming.

inclement exposure. No wonder that it is costly; what abundant reason that it should be rare!'[23]

Indeed, this particular fur achieved such reverence that almost one million animals were slaughtered for fashion and status in just 170 years.

Commercial sea otter hunting had essentially ceased by the twentieth century. The animal had become so rare that the Alaska Commercial Company only found 31 in 1900, despite operating five trading posts and 16 schooners.[24] Many people feared the species had become extinct as a live sea otter had not been seen for such a long time.[25] They were in fact on the brink of extinction with a population lower than 2,000, thinly distributed over 13 remnant colonies. It was only at this near-fatal

Today sea otters are regularly hunted by tourists and shot with their cameras. This photograph was taken in Morro Bay, California.

stage that legislative intervention was taken. In 1911 the organized killing finally ended when the United States, Russia, Great Britain and Japan agreed the Fur Seal Treaty. This was reinforced in California by federal law in 1913. Under these enactments the sea otter gained legal protection across the world for the first time in its history. During the twentieth century these laws were strengthened in the United States (Marine Mammal Protection Act, 1972; Endangered Species Act, 1973)[26] and Canada (Special at Risk Act, 2002). The fur trade also became more strongly regulated in 1975 when the Convention on International Trade in Endangered Species of Wild Fauna and Flora (CITES) was agreed. The southern sea otter was identified as endangered, and added to Appendix I of the treaty with the giant, marine, neotropical, southern river, and a subspecies of the Eurasian otter. These species gained full protection against the commercial fur trade. Every other otter was considered threatened and listed in Appendix II, which allows regulated harvests and licensed trade if national legislation permits.[27]

The species has gone on to make a remarkable recovery. The northern sea otter now has an estimated population of between 64,600 and 77,300. The Russian subspecies has increased to approximately 15,000; and the southern sea otter, once feared extinct, has grown to 2,800.[28] Today the devastation of commercial hunting seems like a distant memory, especially as the species faces a new range of threats (see chapter Seven). Yet despite this, the most luxuriant fur in the world still has its admirers. In 2005 300 sea otter pelts were sold on the black market in Petropavlovsk-Kamchatsky, and a further 300 were sold illegally in Moscow.[29] More recently there was controversy in Canada when the Nuu-chah-nulth Tribal Council announced their plan to re-establish hunting off the coast of Vancouver Island, on the grounds of it being an 'aboriginal right'. If approved by the Canadian government one per cent of the territory's sea otters will be killed for ceremonial purposes, amounting to roughly 20 animals a year. Although there is opposition, the Tribal Council president insists that any killing will be cultural, rather than commercial: 'For us, it's not about the numbers. It's about reconnecting with the pelts worn by our chiefs, the heads of our governments.'[30]

4 Otter Hunting for Sport

For centuries the otter was killed in Britain for its fish-eating ways. By the nineteenth century the animal was increasingly valued as a gallant sporting adversary, and otter hunting achieved a particular fashion and vogue. Hunts with formalized organizational structures, rules, uniforms and territories sprung up on river valleys across the country. The 15 otter hunts in existence in 1880 had grown to 22 by 1910. In the years to 1939 the number fluctuated between 19 and 26. Each generally had between 100 and 300 subscribers, and on special occasions crowds of over 500 people were recorded. Hunting of otters was relatively popular until 1978, when the otter became a legally protected species.

Historical centres for otter hunting included Wales and the Welsh Borders, south-west and north-west England, and southern Scotland. Otter hunting was by no means standardized or unchanging. Throughout Britain the institutional structures and territorial organization of otter hunts varied greatly. Different people also had different reasons for finding and distinct modes of killing. Until the 1860s all otter hunts were privately owned, many were rather small informal affairs, and none hunted the otter exclusively. There were essentially three types of hunt. The first was the estate pack. These were small and tended to exist at localized levels, hunting waters in and around the estate. A number of important families had hounds and hunt servants in their residence. The Fourth Earl of Aberdeen, George Hamilton-Gordon MP, kept a small pack at Haddo House, for example. The second type was the travelling pack. Although based at an estate, they would take their hounds, by invitation, to any part of the country with the prospect of sport. As a result they travelled great distances and hunted many rivers. Of the earliest travelling packs the most famous belonged to Mr James Lomax. Residing at Clayton Hall, Great Harwood, Lancashire, his home waters were the banks and estuaries of the Hodder, Lune, Ribble and Wyre. Although these waters covered much of Lancashire and parts of Yorkshire and Cumberland, Lomax also ventured to Northumberland, Scotland, Wales and its borders. The third type of hunt was the dual pack. Many sportsmen in Wales and Devon kept hounds, not just to hunt otters, but to hunt whatever wild animal came to hand. Other convenient quarry included the deer, fox, hare, pine marten, polecat and badger.

The season for hunting otters was from April to October. This was not shaped around the breeding habits of the animal. The physical disposition of humans and hounds was the determining factor. As John Henry Walsh stated in *British Rural Sports*: 'No other season but the summer will suit this sport, because the cold water of early spring, winter, or autumn, will chill and cramp hounds and men to a dangerous degree.'[1] During the summer months the otter held an unrivalled status in the hunting calendar. As the century progressed more and more sportsmen became solely devoted to hunting this animal.

The sport attracted people from different social and economic backgrounds. In Northumberland otter hunting was predominantly a working man's pastime, enjoyed by farmers, innkeepers, tailors, shoemakers, joiners and blacksmiths. This was much the same in Carlisle. Here the local people liked the sport so much that they set up the first subscription pack in

1864. As an official hunt club all members paid a subscription, the master and committee controlled the club, and a paid huntsman was responsible for the hounds. For a small donation, non-subscribers were also openly welcomed.

The Hawkstone OH (est. 1870) in Shropshire, on the other hand, was an aristocratic hunting club. Subscription fees remained high to keep it exclusive. The Crowhurst OH (est. 1903) was a largely middle-class organization with a female Master, Mrs Mildred Cheesman. This pack was styled as a cosmopolitan hunt within reach of London. Members of the Royal Family were even drawn to the sport. King George V and Queen Elizabeth II each headed the subscription list of the Eastern Counties OH (est. 1898) during their reigns.

Walter Hunt
(1861–1941),
Bolting the Otter,
oil on panel.

By the twentieth century the activity had reached a 'new phase of existence'.[2] In its popular modern form the majority of hunts were financed by subscriptions, meets and hunting calendars were fixed and formalized, packs of hounds had increased dramatically, hunting countries were becoming established, and many packs were solely devoted to killing the otter. The chosen mode of killing had also become standardized. Throughout the nineteenth century there had been two options. The first was by the teeth and jaws of hounds. All otter hunters regarded this method to be legitimate and fair. The second mode of killing involved striking the otter with a barbed spear, known as the otter grain. This was employed in addition to the first mode by some hunts, but was denounced as unfair and illegitimate by others. Although each of these modes led to the same outcome, different otter hunters had different ideas about the legitimacy of killing.

Devotees of spearing regarded their mode of killing as sport, and spears as 'chief requites' for killing.[3] The spear was essentially a strong ashen pole, measuring between six and twelve feet (1.8 to 3.6 m) in length, shod with a sharp iron head. Transfixing

Engraving by William Daniell, from his *Interesting Selections from Animated Nature*, 1809.

65

the otter was seen as the most sportsmanlike and fair method. Not only did it allow the otter to die fighting, it prevented the hounds from getting mauled. Perhaps most importantly, as 'a good worry' was considered to be an 'animated part of the hunt'; this ritual was also relished as the concluding spectacle of death.[4] Spear packs generally took a utilitarian stance. This was largely informed by the public perception of otter as fish-killer. In order to deter riparian owners, pisciculturists and anglers from freely killing the animal, otter hunters had to publicize their intent to kill, and the spear was an obvious symbol of this. Sir Edwin Landseer's dramatic painting *The Otter Hunt* is a classic depiction of the practice. Painted in 1844, it shows the huntsman of the Earl of Aberdeen's OH surrounded by his baying pack, triumphantly holding aloft the impaled otter that adorns his spear. Beside the riverbank lay two dead fish, justification for the killing.

Spearing was also a ritualistic rite of passage. It required strength, agility, endurance, perseverance and precision. In 1835 a youthful William Pook Collier, aged only fifteen, gained permission from his father to take control of his pack for just one day. After only two hours on the River Yarty, William had speared his first otter, weighing 24 lbs (10.9 kg). To honour this achievement, the otter was stuffed, a celebratory dinner was held, and the hunt's president officially initiated William as a member of the Culmstock Society of Otter Hunters.[5] This form of initiation was still prevalent in the late nineteenth century. On 1 May 1869, Captain Edwards, Master of the Dewsland OH of Pembrokeshire, played a prominent role in spearing the otter:

> At last a successful thrust was made by the captain. The depth of the water and strength of the animal were too much for the arms of the spearman, who became twice submerged; still he held on his victim and lifted him to the top of the water, and partly out, cheered by the company.[6]

This was acknowledged as the best sport ever witnessed by everyone involved. High praise, considering Edwards came from a non-spear pack and had never speared an otter before.

By the twentieth century these skills were no longer valued; non-spearing otter hunters had gradually become increasingly accepted and embraced as model sportsmen. In the 1849 *Guide to Foxhounds, Staghounds, Harriers and Otter Hounds*, for instance, the huntsman who received highest praise, Mr Lomax, had shunned artificial aids since establishing his pack in 1829. The section dedicated to his pack read: 'No hounds or man in England understand the habits of the otter better than Mr Lomax and his hounds. He has killed the amphibious animal from Lancashire to Lands End, and uses neither net, spear, nor any other warlike engines, save horn and hound, in pursuit of his game.'[7] This disapproval of 'warlike engines' was increasingly vocalized as the nineteenth century progressed. More often than not their absence was used to underline the high level of skill and sportsmanship that a huntsman had.

The hunting experience also became more important than the need to kill. William Turnbull, a member of the Bellingham OH (1850s–60) and John Gallon's OH (1830–73), emphasized this point in his 1896 publication *Recollections of an Otter-Hunter*. Counteractive strategies were often taken to ensure a good day's sport: 'We invariably tried to capture the otter, instead of killing him, and never destroyed a female, as a hunt could afterwards be arranged and friends invited.'[8] If females were 'never destroyed' they could, in theory, continue to breed and thus maintain a population to be hunted. Similarly, if an otter was captured rather than killed, its presence was ensured for the next hunt. This meant that the laborious process of finding could instantly be exchanged for the excitement of the chase or even the conclusive scene of 'fair combat'. This was a sure-fire way of showcasing a pack, displaying skills such as tailing, and impressing distinguished 'friends'. In his *Diary of Otter Hunting, from AD 1829 to 1871*, James Lomax also made it clear that the lives of otters were intentionally spared on a regular basis. Throughout his diary there are countless entries noting how hounds were 'called off for fear of killing'.[9] Although Lomax rarely justifies these actions explicitly, his words, like Turnbull's, often reveal an ongoing consideration for future sport.

When new packs emerged they chose not to adopt the spear. Its use dwindled and its adherents disappeared as hunts disbanded and packs changed hands. The Wooler OH of Northumberland, for example, disbanded in the late 1860s. When Sir Rowland Hill's OH was taken over by his brother Geoffrey in 1869, he chose not to adopt the spear. The Cheriton OH decided to abandon the spear in 1874, soon followed by the Dartmoor OH in 1876. Mr Collier's OH was last to give to up in 1884, 'as his field did not care to see so gallant a beast suffer such an end'.[10] By the twentieth century most otter hunters spoke of the 'remote and barbarous days of the spear',[11] and broadly disregarded spearing as one of the 'blood-thirsty methods used by our forefathers'.[12] The end of spearing brought the standardization of killing. With this, the type of dogs selected to hunt otters became more important, and the number of hounds used in a pack increased. In 1842, for example, Grantley Berkeley, the man who was described as the 'best of modern otter-slayers and the most experienced authority on the sport',[13] had a pack that consisted of four old foxhounds, three white terriers, and several men armed with spears. As the century progressed packs grew and the prominent pedigrees consisted of either foxhounds, otterhounds, crossbred hounds, or a mixture of each. By 1910 all packs comprised of between ten and twenty-five couples.

To the dedicated otter hunter the sport was superior to any other. Yet according to certain authorities only one-tenth of the hunting fraternity transferred themselves to the sport.[14] This was directly tied to the environment in which the otter lived. The only way to follow hounds through watery terrains was by foot. The absence of horses was an unattractive prospect to

anyone who hunted to ride. Foxhunter Sir W. Beach Thomas (1936) made this point in *Hunting England*: 'the votaries of otter hunting are relatively few, for the very good reason that in fox- and stag-hunting the horse is at least as important as the hound or the quarry.'[15] This horselessness informed the pace of the pursuit. The exhilarating speed of riding to hounds was replaced with a moderate to brisk walking pace. Otter hunting was promoted as a healthy and refreshing sport. It offered a day of hard exercise, which could last between five and seven hours and cover distances from three to thirty miles (4.8 to 48 km). The pursuit was not confined to the riverbanks; hounds frequently led followers through and across the water. An otter hunter was therefore expected to leap over brooks, stand in streams, trudge across muddy bogs, wade in rivers and stomp through tangled undergrowth. These conditions attracted a certain type of sportsman, hardy individuals with distinctive sporting tastes. As Douglas Macdonald Hastings wrote in the *Picture Post* in

1939: 'To qualify as a follower of otter hounds, it is necessary to be blessed with seal-like imperviousness to water; an affection for muddy places; and the urge to out-walk a hiking club.'[16]

The pedestrian nature of the sport meant otter hunting was affordable and inclusive. The kit and equipment required was minimal and relatively inexpensive. The workmanlike clothes consisted of woollen serge and flannel garments: cap, coat, jacket, shirt, knickerbockers and hose. There was no need for extravagant accessories, a 'good pair of legs', 'thick pair of boots'[17] and serviceable pole was the only requirement. Meets were colourful occasions, with packs creating their own unique fashions. Mr Collier's OH is a fine example. From as early as 1817 those involved with the pack wore: 'a scarlet coat . . . with blue and white flannel trousers and waistcoat, the blue lines running around the legs, and a black bowler hat. The kennel huntsman wore an otter-skin cap with the rudder fastened in front with the hunt button.'[18] This combination of colour and carcass was unlike that of any other. Other packs made more subtle references. The Carlisle OH incorporated the working dress of butchers, a blue-and-white

The Hawkstone OH drawing rough country on the River Teifi, near Lampeter.

striped waistcoat, into their uniform as some of its co-founders came from that trade. Combinations of blue, white, yellow, grey and green were not out of place along the riverbanks.

Otter hunting was not just an excuse to wear costumes and have a stroll in the country. It was a serious matter. Before an otter could be hunted it had to be found. With no fixed home their whereabouts were shrouded with mystery. Any sheltered hollow could be a temporary residence. The animal was therefore largely unseen in the landscape. There were visual clues. The five-toed impressions of webbed feet ('spur', 'seal' or 'mark'), the animal's excrement ('spraint', 'wedging' or 'coke'), and the remains of partially eaten fish each provided confirmation of a former presence. This did not, however, provide precise locations. The only way an otter could be found was by tracing its enduring trail of scent ('line', 'drag' or 'trail'). As with all forms of hunting scent was difficult to interpret and its quality was affected by a range of conditions. High winds, direct sunlight, high humidity and cold

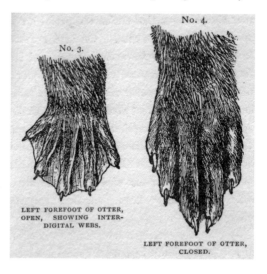

The Eurasian otter is an elusive species. Their former presence can be revealed by impressions left beside the water by their webbed feet.

No. 3.

No. 4.

LEFT FOREFOOT OF OTTER, OPEN, SHOWING INTERDIGITAL WEBS.

LEFT FOREFOOT OF OTTER, CLOSED.

72

air accounted for bad scent. Olfactory remnants also deteriorated with time. Hunting started early in the morning for this reason. The actual scent of the otter was less mysterious than other hunted animals. Its movement between land and water meant that drops of scent-carrying water were left on the ground. Hounds could trace this with relative ease. The relationship between scent and water was far less reliable. The watery landscape was always in motion. Currents and erratic flows carried scent. If an otter entered flowing water the buoyant remnants were by no means coherent or conclusive. It was confirmation of a former presence, but did not necessarily provide an otter. This undoubtedly confused the noses of the hounds. The uncontrollable environment made the process of bringing about the presence of an otter very difficult. It also raised the perceived complexity of the activity, and elevated ideas of the skilled sportsman.[19]

A hunted otter seeks refuge beneath the supported banks of the River Otter, Devon.

As the otter had the opportunity to disappear back into its watery environment, otter hunting was often likened to 'a glorified game of hide and seek'.[20] When a pack of hounds searched for an otter's trail they were encouraged 'to examine . . . every likely-looking place . . . over and over again'.[21] This thorough approach ensured that the followers remained at close proximity to the hounds. Although houndwork was important throughout hunting cultures, it was particularly valued in otter hunting. 'The true otter hunter', wrote Neale in 1950, 'loves to see hounds working out the overnight drag of their quarry, and many a sportsman can derive as much delight and enjoyment from this age-old instance of the mystery of hunting by scent as he may from the pursuit of the otter itself.'[22] Experienced huntsmen interpreted the sounds and movements of the dogs. Every possible situation could be translated. For example, if the trail did not lead to an otter, the quarry could be 'out of mark', that is, residing in a holt with an underwater entrance which concealed its scent from the outer air. Alternatively, the hounds might have 'flashed over' or 'passed over' the drag. This could happen through the pack's eagerness, with hounds overrunning the line at speed. Otter hunters therefore styled themselves as perceptive individuals who understood an older and more authentic style of hunting.[23]

The unique composition of every pack contributed to this. Different breeds of dog had different qualities, including strength, stamina, speed, voice, marking ability and appearance. Otter hunters became accustomed to the particular attributes of their working pack. As these characteristics directly contributed to both the experience and the aesthetic of otter hunting, opinions on which type of hound was best suited to hunt the otter were often quite different. There was a distinct regional variation in the selected blend of breeds. William Pook Collier, who was Master of the Culmstock OH from 1837 to 1890, was particularly intrigued by this. Shortly before retiring from his 43-year mastership, he had declared that, 'in all his experience of otter hunting he had never seen an otterhound', but 'hoped to have a day with one of the more northern packs in order to see what they were like'.[24] Arthur Heinemann of the Cheriton OH was also drawn to these regional differences. In 1903 he claimed that: 'North countrymen prefer the rough hound, west countrymen the smooth.'[25] These preferences primarily reflected ownership and projected self-identity. Surprisingly, the otterhound had its critics. The breed was not considered to be hardy enough for the sport. This claim was to a certain extent informed by the animal's rough coat. When its long hair got soaked with water it took longer to dry; this made it susceptible to chills, which in turn led to its irritability and short temper. The weight of the excess water was also believed to induce fatigue at a relatively early stage. Despite these shortcomings, critics did appreciate

The Dumfriesshire OH were staunch supporters of the otterhound. When the hunt formed in 1889 one of its chief aims was to breed the perfect dog for hunting otters. After selective breeding they were certain the otterhound was superior to all other dogs.

certain qualities. Aubyn Trevor-Battye, for instance, wrote that: 'Every master of Otter-hounds would, no doubt, like to have some of these beautiful hounds in his pack, but the fact is this: the fox-hound does the work better.'[26] As the breed started to dwindle in the 1920s, this appreciation of the aesthetic of the otterhound was increasingly publicized. For many people, it was looked upon as a living relic of the sport's romanticized past. Kathleen F. Barker was one such person. In her 1939 publication, *The Young Entry,* she wrote: 'To me otter-hunting possesses a flavour reminiscent of other older and more gracious days . . . particularly . . . when the hounds are of the pure, rough-coated variety.'[27]

Followers could also play an important role in finding the otter. A knowledgeable field was fully aware of the importance of seeing and doing. Everyone was expected to actively assist the hounds. It was important that people spread out along the riverside. With all eyes focused on the water there were a number of

Members of the Crowhurst OH form a perfect stickle.

signs to look for. If the otter was swimming deep under water, air bubbles from its fur often rose to the surface and produced a 'chain' of bubbles. When swimming closer to the surface, such movements were more likely to cause a wave. It may 'vent', that is, take in air by pushing its snout above the water. It may be viewed in clear water, or even take to the land. Actually knowing whether the otter had really been 'gazed' was often considered as one of most difficult parts of otter hunting. Once the otter had been found there was the distinct possibility it would escape. A device known as the 'stickle' was used to help avoid this. When instructed by the huntsman, men, women and children would wade into the river and form a line from one bank to the other. Standing conjoined they would then use their poles to splash the water. This bodily barrier aimed to prevent the animal from going upstream ('top stickle') or downstream ('bottom stickle'). If successful, the otter would change direction and return to the hounds.[28]

Mr Courtenay Tracy retrieves the dead otter from the hounds.

These participatory practices clearly set otter hunting apart from other forms of hunting. The inclusiveness heightened a sense of belonging. The close proximity positioned the bodies and prepared the eyes for the kill. Although there were individuals who claimed the quarry 'should always be allowed to escape',[29] killing was the intended conclusion. It marked the end of the cultural event. The spectacle itself was a frenzy of frothing water, barking hounds, excitement, tension, teeth, flesh and blood. Hunt-staff were also involved. They used their hands, knees and poles to retrieve the dead otter from the pack. This culminated in a moment of display and symbolism. The huntsman would ceremoniously raise the otter above his head in clear view of the spectators. The carcass was then weighed, recorded and dismembered. Once removed, the mask, rudder and pads could be distributed as trophies; visceral reminders of the day. Newcomers would also be initiated into the hunt with the blooding of forehead, cheeks and chin. At the finish, the body was thrown to the pack and the horn was blown to announce that a kill had been scored.[30]

The unseen nature of the otter meant that this spectacle did not always take place. The chances of seeing one was considerably less than even, and if found roughly half would go on to escape. This uncertainty enhanced ideas of fair play; however, blank days were not embraced. For cynics, hunting without an otter was a sport without a purpose, an activity to be smugly disregarded. The satiric press often parodied this criticism. Otter hunters responded by promoting broader aspects of their sport: 'in otter hunting, the hounds, the invigorating air of the early morning, and the superb beauty of England's valleys and dales constitutes the chief attractions . . . the quarry itself is quite a secondary consideration.'[31] The role of the otter and its death was underplayed. Instead the season, settings, time of meet and pace of pursuit were valued. Otter hunting was styled as a leisurely pastime which encouraged social intercourse and offered relaxation. An intriguing part of this was the lunchtime interval. After long summer mornings afoot, a short break for food and light refreshments was an eagerly awaited event. Although unscheduled, blank mornings, long drags and kills were all suitable circumstances. During this pause, the river provided all the essential amenities for resting. The grassy verges and wooden fence-rails which lined the riverside facilitated tired legs, wide-spreading trees offered shelter from the sunshine (or indeed the rain), and the banks themselves allowed followers to sit with their feet dangling in the cool, plashing water.

Although newcomers were often surprised that an otter hunt could resemble a giant picnic, it was by no means a novelty. Food and fraternizing had been integral since the 1830s. In July 1835, for instance, a member of the Dartmoor Otter Hounds wrote in his diary: 'found above Plym Bridge and had him up two or three hours, but did not kill, as the pretty girls and the picnic spread engaged the hearts of the gallants and the hungry ones.'[32] Although some felt this leisurely dimension detracted from the sport, others saw it as the main attraction. Jack Ivester Lloyd underlined this point in 1952: 'In the days before 1939, when food was plentiful and in amazing variety, I believe that a few people actually paid their subscriptions, drove many miles to meets, wandering down mill lanes and over hump-backed bridges just because the sport gave them an excuse to picnic by the river with other cheery folk.'[33] The one thing that all otter

Members of the Cheriton OH follow hounds at a leisurely pace along the River Taw, North Devon.

hunters agreed was that the endless variety and beauty of the river valleys could never disappoint.

Otter hunting was not welcomed by everyone. Those opposed to blood sports believed it was cruel and called for its abolition. Otter hunters were described as barbaric and vile. The Humanitarian League initiated the campaign against the sport at the beginning of the twentieth century. This was continued by the League for the Prohibition of Cruel Sports (LPCS) and National Society for the Abolition of Cruel Sports (NSACS) from the 1920s, and the Hunt Saboteurs Association (HSA) in the 1960s and '70s. Although they had different strategies their shared objective was to raise awareness by exposing the cruelties involved.

Initially campaigners bombarded newspapers and magazines with letters of protest. These tactics were deployed in July 1905 when the press reported an incident that became known as the Barnstaple cat-worrying case. In this case, which was brought by the RSPCA, the Master of the Cheriton Otter Hounds, Walter Lorraine Bell, and three of its members were found guilty of charges relating to cruelty to cats. The incident horrified the public. The otter hunters involved had been using cats to train their young terriers to 'bolt' otters in a specially constructed wooden tunnel. Although the cruelty was not disputed, Bell's defence to the charge showed little remorse. First, he insisted that cats had been used, as he could not always get hold of a badger. Second, he felt that as he had bought the cats they were his own property. And third, he argued that it was less cruel to use a cat than a badger as worrying the latter badly injured the dogs.[34] Bell was sentenced to one month's imprisonment with hard labour. John Church, the Hunt's Whip, received half that sentence. Having been allowed bail, the pair's charges were later revised on appeal to a £5 fine, on the understanding that Bell gave a donation of £100 to the North Devon Infirmary.

The Humanitarian League's reaction to this case was interesting. Rather than focusing solely on the incident, they redirected their attention to the public's response to it. This allowed broader questions to be raised. Ernest Bell, no relation to the prosecuted, carefully used this formula in the *Animals' Friend* journal soon after the prosecution: 'It is quite right that the press should express horror at such barbarity, but after all in what respect is the deliberate worrying of otters for amusement any less cruel or reprehensible than the worrying of cats. As long as the former is held to be legitimate sport, the latter is likely to appear highly amusing to the sportsmen.'[35] For Bell, the only difference between an otter and a cat was their legal status. He wanted society to step back and reconsider the moral distinction between wild and domestic animals. Alongside this broad criticism, the incident was also used to expose the behaviour of 'sportsmen' in general. Bell argued that it offered an insightful 'glimpse into the mind of the sporting man',[36] and provided further evidence of 'the barbarous spirit engendered by indulgence in blood sports'.[37] In these terms, this exceptional incident was absorbed into the broader campaign against blood sports.

In 1906 League members used a larger institution to elevate their campaign. During the RSPCA's 82nd Anniversary meeting on 21 May, Stephen Coleridge unexpectedly proposed that the committee should prepare a bill to make otter hunting illegal. As the RSPCA did not oppose blood-sports this proposal was a radical move. The fact that otter hunting was singled out suggests that Coleridge felt this particular activity was vulnerable enough to be prohibited. Coleridge recounted the moment when he first witnessed an otter hunt:

The miserable little animal was pursued by men with large poles with spikes in their heads . . . Then the poor creature having found refuge in its hole, twenty men got on to the bank and endeavoured by jumping and other means to force the earth down into the unfortunate animal's hiding place, and this 'sport' was continued, until worn out by fatigue and fright surrounded by men and dogs, without the ghost of a chance of escape, the victim became as easy prey to its enemies.[38]

The audience recoiled in horror, supporting the speaker with shouts of 'Shame!' After much perseverance by Coleridge, the chairman eventually agreed to put the resolution to the meeting. The motion was supported and the resolution was carried with acclamation. This approval was a remarkable success. It immediately generated adverse reactions and increased press coverage. The *Daily Mail*, for instance, received several telegrams from Masters of Otter Hounds opposing Mr Coleridge's criticism and justifying their sport. Mr Rose of the Eastern Counties OH described the proposed Bill as 'most unfair and ridiculous'. He also argued that the description of otter hunting was 'grossly misrepresented'. This opposition to the Bill was surprisingly effective. After only two months the ongoing pressure proved too much and the bill was exposed as an empty promise. In July 1906 the journal *Animal World* announced that the committee was not prepared to take any action on the motion moved by Stephen Coleridge with regard to otter hunting.

LPCS members started taking more direct action in the 1930s, with public protests at otter hunts. The first took place on 28 April 1931, when a small group assembled at Islip to demonstrate against the Buckinghamshire OH. Although this demonstration was by all accounts 'quiet and orderly', the encounter did produce a newsworthy spectacle.[39] As the otter hunters arrived, the group of men and women formed a barrier across the bridge.

Armed with placards, banners and leaflets, they were determined to stand in their path. Their message was clear: 'Abolish the Shameful Sport of Otter Hunting'. After some lively verbal exchanges between the Master and demonstrators, the chief protester, Mrs Chapman, attempted to address the crowd by standing on a chair. This act of individual defiance was soon silenced by the laughter of the unreceptive audience. With this, the interlude faded and the hunting got back under way. When the HSA formed in 1963 they adopted more disruptive measures, sabotaging hunts by laying false scent trails,[40] sounding hunting horns, blocking roads, and actively resisting. On occasion this ended with violent clashes.[41]

The perceived cruelty of otter hunting, as with any given blood sport, was directly tied to the physical characteristics of the animal involved, and the environment in which it was pursued and killed. Otter hunting was considered one of the cruellest blood sports. Invariably, aspects lauded by otter hunters, such as seasonality, the duration of hunts, inclusiveness and involvement in and engagement with the kill, were translated into cruelties peculiar to the sport.

Where the seasonality of the practice was conducive to leisure for otter hunters, its correspondence with the breeding season

Leeds League Members protesting against the Kendal & District OH in 1935.

HSA (Hunt Saboteurs Association) members sabotaging an otter hunt in the 1970s.

Eurasian otter cub.

and the pursuit of pregnant otters was seen as a mark of cowardice. Campaigners repeatedly pointed to this subject as proof of the 'inconsistency and heartlessness'[42] of the hunting fraternity. As this practice was almost exclusively[43] reserved to otter hunting, they also tried to divide the hunting fraternity by distinguishing the sporting conduct of otter-hunters from fox-hunters, stag-hunters and hare-hunters: 'If the sporting set consider it unsporting to hunt some animals in the breeding season, why does this not apply to otters?'[44] For campaigners, the killing of defenceless cubs and their mothers was the antithesis of fair play, sportsmanship and manliness. Justification for killing was also repeatedly questioned. Bertram Lloyd urged the public to make up their own mind: 'If otters are really pests, as it is often pretended, to hunt them during the breeding season would surely be an effective way of exterminating the species. If they are not pests, why hunt them at all?'[45] H. E. Bates, the well-known writer about the countryside, made up his mind in 1937:

> Otters are hunted and killed in England, at something
> like the rate of four hundred and fifty a year . . . [I]t means

this: that in my short life of thirty years . . . something
like twelve thousand otters have been killed in England
for the purpose of fun . . . This kind of fun is one of the
reasons why it is so difficult for me, and for that matter
anybody else, to get a sight of an otter.[46]

The duration of hunts was also identified as a particularly cruel
feature. Anti-hunting literature is peppered with articles con-
demning this. For instance, a subsection in the *Hunted Otter*
(1911) titled 'Hunted for Seven Hours' described the lengthy
pursuit of a female otter by the Culmstock OH in 1910. The LPCS
magazine *Cruel Sports* contained an article detailing an 'otter
hunted for nine hours' by the Dumfriesshire OH in 1932. Otter
hunters were attracted to such lengthy hunts as they extended
their day's sport. Campaigners, on the other hand, argued that
the relentless pursuit of one animal for many hours showed a
distinct lack of mercy: 'It is difficult to imagine a more inept
word than "merciful" for a kill at the end of a harrying which
has lasted for many hours!'[47]

The type of people involved in otter hunting and the kind of behaviour it induced also attracted critical attention. Men, women and children could all actively participate in this sport alongside one another. Otter hunters were of course proud of this fact. Opponents were offended by it. Joseph Collinson raised this point in his 1911 pamphlet *The Hunted Otter*:

> A deplorable feature of this sport is that its followers include all sorts and conditions of people: ministers of religion with their wives, young men and young women, sometimes even boys and girls. Not only are they present at these infamous scenes, but, like the huntsmen, are worked up to the wildest pitch of excitement, and join in the final worry and the performance of the obsequies, when the spoils of the chase are distributed.[48]

Ant-bloodsports campaigners did not consider killing animals for sport Christian behaviour. On 26 September 1976 the HSA held a demonstration against Revd Robin Ray, the Master of the Courtenay Tracy OH, Wiltshire.

The scene after a kill. The Bucks OH whipper-in brings a dead otter ashore.

Unlike other blood sports, the main excitement in otter hunting was seen to derive from the involvement in and visual engagement with the visceral spectacle of the kill. If the active roles played by participants in finding the quarry were publicized as signs of inclusiveness and equality, then that meant that everyone involved made a greater contribution to, and was more responsible for, the death of the animal.

The physical characteristics of the otter meant that the 'final worry', much like the preceding pursuit, could be a more prolonged event and more viewable display than scenes that included other hunted animals. In the 1901 publication *British Blood-Sports* Colonel Coulson compared the death of the fox with the death of the otter to emphasize the cruelty of otter hunting:

> In the case of the Fox, few perhaps ever see the death, and it is over almost in an instant. It is not so with the Otter.

Owing to his strength and cat-like tenacity of life he fights long and dies hard. And then everyone can watch, and most do watch, the end . . . people collect from far and near, and there watch in cold blood for minutes together the frantic death-agony of the brave little animal who has never done injury to anyone assembled. It is a brutal, demoralising amusement.[49]

A demonstrator holds a placard depicting the Revd Robin Ray, Master of the Courtenay Tracy OH, as a devil-like figure.

If the strength and combative nature of the otter was regarded as bravery by sportsmen, the mauling inflicted to achieve the kill was said to prolong the animal's suffering. The fact that the otter 'fights long and dies hard' seems to be directed more at the spectator's reaction to the prolonged 'death-agony', than to the actual experience which the animal went through. It appears to be more about human behaviour than animal suffering. Indeed, campaigners believed that the kill had ill effects on the mental well-being of every person involved. According to Coulson, those who engaged in the kill became 'virtually maddened by it'.[50]

For campaigners, the behaviour of otter hunters was uncivilized, un-Christian and un-English. Otter hunting was not a sport or even a form of leisure. It was an activity that facilitated bloodlust. It was not glamorous or romantic. It was not even a true test of physical endurance. Otter hunting was the ruthless torture of a sentient creature. There could be only one explanation for its existence: 'Otters are hunted for one reason only – for the pleasure a hunted Otter gives to the hunter.'[51]

5   The Literary Otter

If the hunted otter was a source of profit, pleasure and protest, the literary otter popularized the animal and widened its audience. Surprisingly, until recent years, the otter rarely featured in mainstream popular literature. Its appearance in some cases was minor. In others it was easily forgotten.[1] There was, however, a small group of authors who were particularly inspired by the animal. Individuals including Henry Williamson, Emil E. Liers and Gavin Maxwell helped to transform the otter into a much-loved fictional and non-fictional character. Its presence in children's literature, nature writing and biographical stories grew as the twentieth century progressed.

Kenneth Grahame introduced the otter to children's literature with his 1908 novel *The Wind in the Willows*. This classic tale recounts the adventures of several riverbank animals in pastoral England. Rat, Mole, Toad and Badger are of course the central characters. Otter also has an important marginal role. Although the animals are anthropomorphized some natural characteristics are retained. Otter makes his first appearance in chapter One. Soon after Mole sees a 'streak of bubbles' on the surface of the water, Otter hauls himself up the bank. After a friendly introduction he tells his friends he was hoping for some privacy: 'Such a rumpus everywhere! . . . All the world seems out on the river today. I came up this backwater to try to get a moment's peace, and then stumble upon you fellows!'[2] When asked who is on the river, Otter mocks the faddish modern ways of a certain individual: 'Toad's out, for one . . . In his brand-new water-boat, new togs, new everything! . . . Such a good fellow, too . . . But no stability – especially in a boat!'[3] Soon after this comment Otter disappears, mid-sentence, back under water.

Otter and his son Portly appear several times in the book. Unlike Rat and Mole, who are content with 'messing about in boats',[4] Otter always wants to do something in the river. Swimming, fishing and indeed disappearing are each mentioned. As well as being a traditional voice for the river community, Otter is also a rugged character with fighting spirit. When Rat and Mole seemingly go missing, but have in fact visited Badger, Otter is at hand to find them. He also escorts the timid pair out of the Wild Wood despite the dangers: 'It'll be all right, my fine fellow . . . I'm coming along with you, and I know every path blindfold; and if there is a head that needs to be punched, you can confidently rely upon me to punch it.'[5]

Grahame also draws on the adventurous and elusive nature of the animal. In 'The Piper at the Gates of Dawn,' baby Portly goes missing for a number of days. Otter is left worried and anxious about his son. In this magical chapter Rat and Mole paddle upstream through the night in search of the youngster. When they hear mysterious pipe music playing they cannot help but follow. Much to their surprise this leads them to a mystical demigod, a friend and helper to little animals. Between his hooves they find Portly sleeping soundly. Once Portly is safely reunited with his father he is not mentioned again in the novel. His inclusion closely associated otters with family, mysticism and mystery.

American naturalist Thornton W. Burgess (1874–1965) was also turning animals into popular children's characters at this time. During his prolific writing career he published over 170 books and 15,000 stories.[6] His writing was entertaining and educational. By remaining faithful to animal behavior he aimed to teach children about nature and conservation. Burgess set his tales in the fictional world of Green Meadows, Smiling Brook and Green Forest. Every animal residing there had their adventures chronicled. Peter Rabbit, Reddy Fox, Grandfather Frog, Buster Bear, Paddy the Beaver, Jimmy Skunk and Old Man

Cover of *Little Joe Otter*, by Thornton W. Burgess, 1935.

Coyote were just a few of the characters. Little Joe Otter made his appearance in 1925.[7]

Little Joe lives with his wife and babies in Laughing Brook. They are styled as a mysterious, unsociable family: 'Little Joe believes that a home is just for those who live there, and therefore it is a secret which no one else should know.'[8] Initially, several residents even question the existence of Mrs Joe, as she

Little Joe Otter and family.

has never been seen. Little Joe is described as a wonderful swimmer and great traveller.[9] As everyone respects his 'sharp, strong teeth', nobody willingly quarrels with him.[10] Each of the 34 chapters begins with a few wise words from Little Joe. These encapsulate the key themes and provide useful moral guidance. In chapters Three, Nine and Nineteen, for example, the words of wisdom read: 'No matter how you love to roam, there comes a time you want a home';[11] ''Tis vain to sit and wish and wish, when fishing where there are no fish';[12] 'True courage ne'er gives way to fear, when unexpected foes appear.'[13] The story itself covers a range of issues. These include learning how to swim, searching for food, the scarcity of fish, the problem with ice, encounters with enemies and the danger of traps. Burgess also introduces children to the harsh realities of American river life. When Yowler the Bobcat decided he wanted otter for dinner, young Otter had to fight for her life: 'He tried to seize her by the throat, but she was too quick for him. The next instant they were rolling over and over in the snow, snarling, spitting, growling, biting and clawing at each other . . . What a fight that was! There was no longer any fear in that young Otter. She was simply fighting mad!'[14] The life of the other young otter is also threatened. He feels the full force of the fur trade when he gets his toe caught in a trap. Little Joe Otter was typically philosophical about the whole situation: 'If life and freedom be the cost, what matter if a toe is lost?'[15]

The animal entered the imaginations of a much larger readership soon after the creation of another fictional otter. The story of *Tarka the Otter: His Joyful Water-life and Death in the Country of Two Rivers* (1927) follows the life of a young otter on the rivers Torridge and Taw in Devon, England. The author, Henry Williamson, describes the habits and experiences of the animal in detail, whilst avoiding sentimentalism. On his two-year journey from birth to death, readers see Tarka learn how to swim, regularly searching for food, interacting with otters, having encounters with wild animals, witnessing the changing seasons, and of course facing the recurring threat of humans and hounds.

In the opening chapter Williamson sets the scene by introducing a female otter, pregnant with Tarka and his two sisters, and the presence of a dreaded scent:

> She stood rigid. The hair on her back was raised . . .
> Mingled with the flower odours, which were unpleasant
> to her, was the taint that had given her a sudden shock
> . . . [T]he taint most dreaded by the otters . . . of the Two
> Rivers – the scent of Deadlock, the great pied hound with
> the belving tongue, leader of the pack whose kills were
> notched on many hunting poles.[16]

Throughout the book, Tarka, like his mother before him, is confronted by the 'dreaded taint' of Deadlock, and the ensuing sight and sounds of otterhounds and otter hunters. On such occasions the protagonist has to run and fight for his life. During each encounter Williamson carefully describes the detailed interaction between the landscape, hunters, dogs and the otter. The story ends with a vivid description of Tarka being hunted for ten hours. Having nearly escaped the bloodthirsty pack, the maimed otter comes face to face with his nemesis, Deadlock:

> Amidst the harsh cries of men and women and the heavy
> tongues of hounds Tarka was overborne by the pack . . .
> Tarka swam down slowly, bleeding from many wounds.
> Sometimes he paddled with three legs, sometimes with
> one, in the water darkening so strangely before his eyes

... At the beginning of the tenth hour ... Hounds were called off by horn, for the tide was at flood. But as they were about to leave, Tarka was seen again, moving with the tide, his mouth open ... Tally-Ho! Deadlock saw the small brown head, and bayed in triumph as he jumped down the bank. He bit the head and lifted the otter high, flung him about and fell into the water with him. They saw the broken head look up beside Deadlock, heard the cry of Ic-yang! As Tarka bit into his throat, and then the hound was sinking with the otter into the deep water ... they waited and watched, until the body of Deadlock arose, drowned and heavy ... They pulled

Young Tarka on the right, wood-engraving by C. F. Tunnicliffe.

the body out of the river and carried it to the bank, laying it on the grass, and looking down at the dead hound in sad wonder. And while they stood there silently, a great bubble rose out of the depths, and broke, and as they watched, another bubble shook the surface, and broke; and there was a third bubble in the sea-going waters, and nothing more.[17]

With this dramatic and saddening climax Williamson not only comments on the harshness of life and nature, but also positions Tarka as a brave and heroic figure.

Williamson's portrayal of the animal was based on hunting knowledge. He first formulated his idea about Tarka having read J. C. Tregarthen's 1909 book, *The Life Story of an Otter*. Williamson felt he 'could improve on the original'.[18] From 1924 he chose to follow his local hunt, the Cheriton Otter Hounds, to gather information. His descriptions of otter hunters were informed by these experiences. Deadlock was also based on the pack's leading hound, Dreamy. Williamson became actively involved in the organization. He met his future wife, Ida Loetitia Hibbert, at an otter hunt, and is thought to have proposed at a Hunt Ball. When the pack's Master, William Henry Rogers, published the Records of the Cheriton Otter Hounds in 1925, Williamson's name appeared in the book's list of subscribers. Rogers was considered such an important influence that Williamson went on to dedicate *Tarka the Otter* to him.

On 12 June 1928 Williamson leapt to fame when he was awarded the Hawthornden Prize for his book.[19] As well as being awarded the princely sum of £100, this honour, perhaps more importantly, generated instant recognition and publicity. In the days following the announcement, the author and Tarka became the subject of national interest. Williamson received

Henry Williamson is presented with the Hawthornden Prize by John Galsworthy on 12 June 1928.

high praise in the press. Many newspapers recited passages from John Galsworthy's presentation speech. *The Times*, for instance, wrote that 'Williamson is the finest and most intimate living interpreter of the drama of wildlife.'[20] The *Daily Telegraph* went into more detail, recounting Galsworthy's explanation:

> If you think of it, when we are interested in beasts and birds and their natural surroundings, it's almost always not for themselves and their good, but for ourselves and our good. We're interested in them commercially; we like to make money out of their feathers and skins . . . or as sportsmen we are terribly fond of some creatures in order to do other creatures in . . . That being so, when a writer can bring to us some true and thrilling sense of the strange, vivid and separate importance of beasts, birds, and plants, shall we not be grateful and do him honour![21]

Cover of *Tarka the Otter*, 1951 edition.

This sentiment soon spread. Williamson's broader work became increasingly appreciated. Tarka became an iconic literary figure. Otter hunting also reached a new popular audience.

Tarka the Otter has been enjoyed by generations of readers across the world. Over the years its popularity has been maintained. Puffin Books reprinted revised editions in 1949, 1951, 1955, 1961 and 1962. A map of Tarka's journey was added in 1963.[22] In 1979 75,000 copies of the Russian edition were printed. English editions have also continued to sell. In 1984 18,000 copies were sold, and a further 11,000 were bought in 1985.[23] For most readers the story makes a lasting impression. British poet Ted Hughes, for example, was fascinated by Tarka. Having first read the book at the age of eleven he turned the pages of little else for a year after. 'It entered into me and gave shape and words to my world, as no book has ever done since',[24] explained Hughes. It later proved an inspiration for his poetry. The poem 'An Otter' features in his 1960 collection *Lupercal*.

The North American river otter was fictionalized in a similar fashion by Emil E. Liers in *An Otter's Story* (1953). This sentimental children's book follows the lives of Ottiga (the Indian name for 'the leader of the herd') and his family on the Mississippi and Wisconsin rivers. Throughout the book their lives are threatened by fisherman, poachers and trappers. By describing their natural ways in the wild, Liers shows how the animal had been 'maligned and misunderstood'.[25] Although stylistically the writing does not compare to that of Williamson, in North America the book raised awareness of otters in a similar way to *Tarka*. This was largely due to the author's unique understanding of the animal. In the 1920s he was a trapper who killed for

Emil Liers with his trained North American otters and dog.

profit. One day when he was collecting a dead female otter from a trap, his life took a dramatic turn. The death had left two young cubs without a mother. The sight of this helpless pair had such an emotional impact that Liers decided to take them home and care for them. He never set another trap.

After this experience Liers continued to adopt and train otters. His aim was to educate the public. He visited schools and conferences. In 1939 Liers took twelve of his pets to Manhattan for the Annual National Sportsmen's Show. This caused quite a stir in the press. *Time* magazine reported:

> There Emil Liers, Minnesota trapper, proudly exhibited his pack of twelve otters, only ones ever bred, raised and trained in captivity. He has taught them to do practically anything otter-hunting dogs can do. The heavy (average: 24 Ibs.), healthy animals perform tricks, follow a scent, retrieve pheasants and ducks with the speed of a prize cocker spaniel.[26]

Liers also set up an otter sanctuary in Homer, Minnesota. 'See the Otters!' signs were put up along the Highway 61 to attract tourists. A small admission fee was charged to help support their upkeep. It was a unique experience. The AAA tour guide of 1946 described it as 'the only trained Otters in the United States'.[27] The key themes in *An Otter's Story* very much brought together the personal experiences and observations of the author. His main intention was to change people's attitudes about the animal. This is made clear in the book's dedication: 'To my friends the otters, with the prayer that the readers of this story may be impressed with the lovableness and intelligence of these little creatures.'[28] The work of Emil E. Liers undoubtedly helped to save the lives of many North American river otters.

While Williamson and Liers fictionalized the wild ways of the animal, the author Frances Pitt (1888–1964) was writing about her domesticated otters. Pitt was very much part of the older amateur natural history tradition. A student of animal psychology and behaviour, she wrote 31 naturalist publications in her lifetime. Pitt believed the best way to learn about otters was to adopt and tame cubs. *Moses, My Otter* (1927) is a biographical story about her relationship with three tame otters, Moses, Aaron and Tom. The book challenges traditional ideas about the animal: 'Reputed savage and morose, long study of my friends has caused me to rate the otter as one of the most intelligent of animals, and only second to the dog in the matter of brains.'[29] Pitt essentially restyles the otter as a loveable pet with brains.

The descriptive writing provides an insight into the ways of the animal. The language used is sentimental at times: the cubs are referred to as 'roly-poly, furry, grey babies'[30] and 'fascinating little people'.[31] The author, who forms a strong emotional bond with her pets, argues that the animals also have feelings for each other. When Aaron elopes with a wild otter, her sister

Frances Pitt described Aaron and Moses as 'two of the most fascinating little people imaginable'.

Frances Pitt, with her pets Tom the otter and Tiny the terrier.

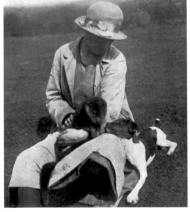

did not react well: 'Poor Moses! She was heart-broken. Never had the cubs been parted . . . Moses smelt at every visiting place, called and cried, but nowhere could she find any trace of the fugitive Aaron! Then Moses came to me, and followed me everywhere, sobbing and crying in a way that tore my heart.'[32] Photographs accompany the text throughout. In one, Pitt is shown sitting on the grass with Tom the otter in her arms and Tiny the terrier laying by her side. The accompanying text reads: 'Tom and Tiny were now the best of friends. All Tom's objections to Tiny had vanished, they went everywhere and did everything together, and, of course, lived and slept together, having the wildest romps around the stable-yard and even about the garden.'[33] This 'friendship' is very different from all other descriptions of otters and dogs at this time. Prior to this publication, the only times these had animals appeared together in a photograph was after blood had been spilled, or was about to be. This bloodless interaction went against all conventional ideas about how these two animals should behave.

On initial reading, one may assume that Pitt's writing played an important role in anti blood-sports rhetoric. One might also conclude that Pitt would have been horrified at the thought of hunting animals to death. This, however, was not the case. Pitt was not a member of the LPCS or NSACS. She did not even oppose blood-sports. She was in fact the Vice President of the British Field Sports Society and a foxhunter. Between 1929 and 1952 Pitt was Master of the Wheatland Hounds though she later became a member of the committee of the Enquiry on Cruelty to Wild Animals, 1949–51.[34] Although Pitt would have served as an excellent example of the inconsistencies of the hunting mind, the anti blood-sports movement chose not to mobilize the sentimental observations of a foxhunter in their case for protecting the wild otter.

Frances Pitt is a fine example of the complex and often contradictory relationship people had with otters. In his 1938 essay, 'On Otters', Henry Williamson criticizes Pitt for her unfavourable review of *Tarka the Otter*:

> A Lady writer and rider to foxhounds, reviewing *Tarka the Otter* in a weekly, complained that the style was 'far from being simple', that 'the Devonshire dialect lays traps for the unwary', that a 'too flowery pen leads the author into many statements which, to put it mildly, are rather rash', and then she goes on to say that the author has never 'known an otter intimately and personally, but has written from otter-hunting experience, and so on.' The critic complains further that Tarka is made 'far too "Hail fellow, well met" with all the other otters on the river'; and then proceeds to say that 'never shall I forget the fury of my old friend Madame Moses when I tried to introduce a dog-cub.' Madame Moses was apparently a tame otter about which a book had been written; and the behaviour of the tame otter made the basis of criticism of wild otters I had observed in their native waters. The lady and fox-hunter concluded by saying that the description of the last hunt was for her 'the most unpleasant of many vivid descriptions.'[35]

This passage shows just how complicated the public image of the otter was.

In 1944 Collins published *The Otter Book* by Phyllis Kelway. This publication bridges the gap between Williamson and Pitt. It sees the author transform from otter hunter to otter protector. While hunting with hounds Kelway had a sudden urge to save a drowning cub. She took extreme measures to save the animal:

I lost my reason, my sense of proportion; but somehow I must save the cub from the death that waited at the weir ...Plunging into the river, I lost sight of the creature I was trying to save; but only for an instant. The splash I made was over, and there, floating away faster now, was the club, its head still turned upstream, its unconquerable spirit shining in those fish-like eyes. I had sufficient sense left to know that I must seize it by the tail.[36]

Kelway nurses the twelve-week-old cub back to good health, names her Juggles, and vows never to hunt again. The book tells the story of the author's Damascene conversion. Kelway and her new pet go on regular excursions along the river over the next year. Danger is never far away. Juggles has a series of close encounters with traps, poison and hounds. Although this charming story is not well known in the twenty-first century, it did make a small impact at the time. Kelway desperately wanted to improve the reputation of wild otters. She domesticated Juggles to start this change: 'I had vowed that if she lived, she should be the means of saving the lives of many otters. People would know her, feel for her as for their own dog, and knowing should be stirred by a twinge of disgust at each kill, which should be the beginning of a new initiation. Juggles had laid the foundations well, but her work had not been finished.'[37]

If the foundations for change had already been laid, the individual ultimately responsible for successfully reconstructing the otter's image was Gavin Maxwell. Maxwell was a Scottish author and naturalist from an aristocratic family. He turned his back on this affluent lineage in favour of a simple life on the West Highland coast. In 1950 he moved to an abandoned house on an isolated beach in Sandaig. He settled there for the next two decades with his pet otters Mijbil, Edal and Teko.[38] In

1960 Maxwell published *Ring of Bright Water*. The novel reflected on his life with otters in a seemingly idyllic setting, Camusfèarna.[39] Although Maxwell described the book as 'a kind of personal diary', critics agree that the narrative was more carefully planned. As Austin Chinn explains, 'he tells true things, but so selected, arranged, and concentrated through literary art that the narrative becomes a kind of fiction'.[40] As well explaining how he was first drawn to otters, he chronicles his growing 'otter fixation',[41] and the joy gained from their companionship. He also recounts amusing anecdotes of outings in London, fondly reflects on his friendships, is deeply saddened by the tragic murder of Mij, and rejuvenated by the adoption of Edal. His surroundings are beautifully described throughout.

The evocative writing and enchanting story had massive popular appeal.[42] The book's introductory sentence brought the reader straight into Maxwell's world: 'I sit in a pitch-pine panelled kitchen-living room, with an otter asleep upon its back among the cushions on the sofa, forepaws in the air, and with the expression of tightly shut concentration that very small babies wear in sleep.'[43] The otter sleeping like a baby was Mijbil. He had been named after an Arab sheikh Maxwell once met. The author's fascination with otters had actually started whilst travelling in the marshes of Southern Iraq. Explorer Wilfred Thesiger had introduced him to the animal and found him his first two cubs. The first, Chahala, died soon after Maxwell adopted her. Maxwell was distraught by the untimely death: 'I killed her by allowing her to eat meat too soon, and I am desolate and full of self reproach. My heart weeps for that curious little otter and I'm very very sad. Now I feel that I shall never be content until I get another.'[44] Several months later contentment arrived in the form a young male cub, Mijbil.

When Maxwell returned to London he was curious to know exactly what type of otter Mij was. The animal seemed unlike any other in natural history literatures. When he visited the London Zoological Society he was pleasantly surprised. It was discovered that Mij was a previously unknown sub-species of smooth-coated otter. As a result of this discovery the sub-species was named after Maxwell, *Lutrogale perspicillata maxwelli.* Maxwell was understandably proud. Since childhood he felt that individuals who gave their name to a species had an air of romance. Steller's sea eagle, Sharpe's crow, Humboldt's woolly monkey and Grant's gazelle all stood out. When Maxwell's otter joined them

Gavin Maxwell with his first otter, Chahala. The photograph was taken in the reed marshes of southern Iraq in 1956.

he felt he 'had realized a far-off childish fantasy'.[45] He later described this as the greatest achievement of his life. This, however, was not celebrated by all. Wilfred Thesiger was baffled that Maxwell had taken the credit:

> I found this otter . . . Gavin wasn't there . . . if it was going to be named after anybody it should have been named after me. Gavin owed everything to this trip with me in the marshes. The marshes gave him the otter, the otter gave him *Ring of Bright Water*, and without that he would never have been heard of again.[46]

As well as success, the otters brought Maxwell happiness. Maxwell was a complicated and troubled man. His sexuality and mental health cast him as an outsider. The constant company and affection demanded by the animal was a welcome distraction. It became his main focus. Otters offered ongoing friendship: 'Mij meant more to me than most human beings.'[47] They went everywhere together, played games, caught fish for each other, slept under the same roof, and even shared a bed. It is this close relationship which makes for such uplifting reading.

Maxwell does anthropomorphize his otters throughout his novels, but is unapologetic for doing so. The appearance of the otter on land was a source of particular amusement. For Maxwell its long tubby torso, short legs, whiskery face and clownish behaviour 'might have been specifically designed to please a child'.[48] When Maxwell lived in London he regularly took Mij out for walks. As would be expected this caused quite a stir. People did not know what the animal was. Stares were followed by questions. These often ranged from the bizarre to the ridiculous. Mij was mistaken for a squirrel, baby seal, beaver, bear cub, leopard, walrus, hippo, newt and even a 'brontosaur'.[49] The

Mij on the steps of
the Maxwell family
estate in Monreith,
Galloway.

level of curiosity and indeed ignorance shows just how little the
British public knew about the otter at this time.

The writing of Maxwell successfully restyled the otter as a
playful and friendly companion. He showed that each of his pet
otters had their own unique personalities. Yet he did not hide
the fact that the otter could not achieve complete domesticity.
Maxwell himself was at the sharp end of a well-intentioned bite
on a few occasions, the most serious of which was administered
by Mij at feeding time. The teeth went through three layers of

gloves, skin and muscle to break two bones in his hand. In *The Rocks Remain* a fifteen-year-old Terry Nutkins did not get off so lightly. This time it was Edal who launched the attack. Nutkins was so badly bitten that he lost two fingers. When the doctor failed in his attempt to save the digits Nutkins was unruffled: 'Chop 'em off, Doctor, that ruddy lot's no good to anyone.'[50] This event did not stop Nutkins caring for animals. He went on to become a successful wildlife expert on British television.

Ring of Bright Water has become one of the most popular wildlife books ever written. In the 1960s it boasted a readership of over one million people. In this time it also topped the US bestseller list for a year and underwent a film adaptation. Today, over two million copies have been sold worldwide. Maxwell's role in promoting the otter cannot be overstated. According to Australian zoologist Peter Crowcroft, 'his was the finest promotion for otters there has ever been'.[51] *Ring of Bright Water*

Gavin Maxwell and Edal resting in the house in Scotland at Sandaig, Isle of Skye, 1960.

Turvy playfully biting Mr Hurrell, from Elaine Hurrell's *Watch for the Otter*, 1963.

'marked the beginning of a groundswell of worldwide support for otter conservation'.[52] By raising awareness on a global scale Maxwell essentially became the spokesman for the species. In doing so, the author became synonymous with the animal: 'Gavin Maxwell was to otters what Joy Adamson was to lions, Diane Fossey to gorillas, Jane Goodall to chimpanzees and Grey Owl to beavers.'[53]

As the public became more interested in the otter, the animal made more appearances in popular literature. A string of books were written about domesticated otters. Readers were introduced to an array of fascinating characters. Juggles, Mij, Edal and Teko were joined by Ingo, Topsy, Turvy, Oswald, Okee, Beever, Limpet, Ripple, Gutsy, Rhona, Rhum, Kate, Lucy, Fury, Freckie, Kuala, Mango, Stinkerbelle and Bee.[54] The animal also continued to inspire authors to write fictionalized stories.[55] Joseph A. Davis, for example, added the spotted-necked otter to fiction with *Samaki, the Story of an Otter in Africa*. Set on a Tanzanian river, this *Tarka*-esque tale follows the life of Samaki. During the adventure, mongooses, leopards, elephants, crocodiles and hippos are all seen as potential dangers.

Children's fiction has also embraced the animal. In the past few decades children have become spoilt for choice with otter titles. Enjoyable reads range from Joe Barber-Starkey's *Jason and the Sea Otter* (1997) to Jill Tomlinson's *The Otter Who Wanted to Know* (2004).[56] The ever-popular Winnie-the-Pooh has also been joined by a new friend, Lottie the Otter, in the long-awaited

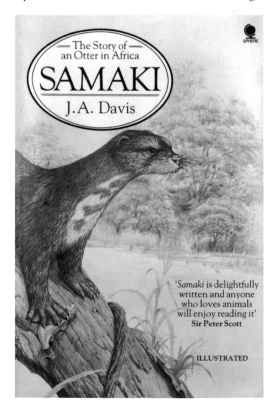

— The Story of —
an Otter in Africa
SAMAKI
J. A. Davis

'Samaki is delightfully written and anyone who loves animals will enjoy reading it'
Sir Peter Scott

ILLUSTRATED

Cover of *Samaki*, by J. A. Davis, 1979.

Return to the Hundred Acre Wood (2009). This feisty character is sure to become a favourite. The literary otter has not only transformed the animal into much-loved fictional and non-fictional characters, but has also popularized the species amongst generations of readers and initiated a movement towards its own protection.

6 The Otter On Screen

The otter has been the focus of folkloric stories for centuries. It has been depicted in natural history publications and popularized by the literary otter. Despite this, until recently very few people had actually seen moving images of the animal. The otter first appeared on television and cinematic screens in the 1960s. Film adaptations of novels and children's television programmes brought the animal to life. With this new-found voice and presence the otter became an iconic on screen character.

Walt Disney Ltd first showed their interest in adapting *Tarka the Otter* into a film in June 1957. When they approached Henry Williamson to buy the copyright the author politely declined. According to Anne Williamson, his daughter-in-law and biographer, Henry did not believe his story would be faithfully retold: 'He thought that Disney was actually going to make the film based on a very inferior American book which had already plagiarised Tarka.'[1] Although any accusations of plagiarism are debatable, Williamson's underlying concern was confirmed. On 30 April 1961 *Flash, the Teen-age Otter* was aired on ABC in America.[2] The 50-minute television film was based largely on Emil E. Liers book *An Otter's Story*. Rutherford Montgomery was responsible for re-writing the film script.[3] The screenplay followed the same format as other nature documentaries in Disney's true life adventure series: real animals were accompanied with a fictional narrative, a medley of classical music and anthropomorphic humour. For Walt Disney, it was the humanlike personality of animals which entertained audiences.

The story is about a family of otters. Lutra, Grey Muzzle, and their cubs Fleta and Flash live beside an old mill pond in Wisconsin. As their home is within a wildlife reserve they live in relative safety, protected from people. This sanctuary is styled as an 'otter's playground', a place to safely play 'games of tag, follow the leader, seek and find'. When they travel beyond this protection the natural curiosity of Flash separates him from his family. The young otter falls into a fast-flowing river and gets swept away. The audience is told that Flash is struck with 'fear and loneliness'. He immediately encounters death when he comes across a lifeless female otter killed by a trap. Humans are very much cast as the enemy; the menace is never far away. Flash, and travel companion Tina, endure a series of life-threatening incidents, the first of which shows the title character getting caught in a fisherman's net. The only reason the otter is not killed on the summer day is because a winter pelt was worth more. With his life valued at $40, Flash gets 'a stay of execution' and is imprisoned in a chicken coop. The fisherman's intention is made quite clear. After a panning shot of pelts hanging on a rack the man sharpens his knife and readies his wooden pole. The narrator calmly states: 'There was no sentiment here. This was business. Flash was just a piece of merchandise to be disposed of at the most profitable time. That time was now.' Fortunately for Flash, who has good fortune on his side, this does not prove to be the case. He makes a swift escape, only to end up in another danger zone. This time he is confronted by the hooked bait of anglers, the shotgun of a gamekeeper, and the jaws of two dogs. Again he bravely fights for his life and gets away unscathed.

The final encounter between Flash and a human sees a change in his luck. When a trap snaps shut around the young otter some viewers may fear for his life. Is this the end? Is Flash dead? As would be expected, there is a twist in the tale. The live trap, set to prevent injury, belonged to the State Conservation Department. They are not interested in killing the animal but rather reintroducing it to the wildlife reserve.[4] With this moral turn the viewing public is shown they have a choice. People do not have to be the enemy; they can choose which relationship to have with the otter. The personality of Flash is persuasive. Despite facing ongoing adversity he remains 'joyous, fun-loving' and 'care-free'. His general behaviour and interaction with animals is particularly endearing. He plays with young raccoons until the odorous skunk spoils their fun, he befriends goats, and entertains the audience by becoming 'a dancing otter'. He even enjoys tobogganing in the snow. Then of course there is the proverbial happy ending, where Flash is reunited with his family and travel companion. With these heartwarming scenes the narrator describes otters as 'the happiest animals in nature'. This combination of entertainment and education projected a favorable identity onto the creature. The anthropomorphic sentimentalism undoubtedly convinced millions of viewers to change their opinion of the animal.

During the filming process the behaviour of 'Flash' was quite different. Montgomery, the scriptwriter, reflected on this. Although he was pleased with the acting ability of the otters, he felt their on-screen presence needed attention: 'They make fine actors but they kept the cameraman in a tizzy because they never pause long enough for a pose or reaction shot. Quite often the scenes would arrive at the studio and . . . there was no otter in the frame at all.'[5] Surprisingly, several cast members would have welcomed such an absence. Two large dogs shared a number of scenes with the otter. They were meant to fiercely attack the animal. Although the crew ensured no harm would be done to the animals, the otter definitely made an impression: 'The dogs eagerly leaped into the water to attack. Within a few minutes they were crawling up the bank, completely licked by one small, muzzled otter. It was impossible to get them out of their crates for a re-take. They cowered there until the otter was taken away.'[6] The natural instincts of the animal could not be hidden despite the character's cute and cuddly persona.

Otters finally made their much-anticipated debut on the cinema screen in 1969. Filmmakers were interested in *Ring of Bright Water* before the book had even been published.[7] British producer Michael Powell acquired film rights after reading a proof copy in 1959. This was taken over by American producer Joseph Strick some years later. Filming started in 1967 with Jack Couffer as director. Couffer had previously been a director and

Graham Merrill, played by Bill Travers, with Mij the otter.

cameraman for Walt Disney Wildlife Productions. Bill Travers and wife Virginia McKenna were cast as the lead roles. Just three years earlier they had starred together in the award-winning film *Born Free*. As well as being a box-office hit, this adaptation of Joy Adamson's book raised global awareness for lion conservation. *Ring of Bright Water* would have an even greater influence on otter protection.

Main character Mij 'was clearly the star of the show'.[8] A variety of otters were cast in the leading role, and each had their own unique personality. The actors struck up quite a friendship with them. McKenna and Travers had, of course, befriended lions during *Born Free*. McKenna revealed the same method was used with the otters: 'Bill and I sat in a large hillside enclosure with a stream running below and the otter ('Mij') splashed in the water and scampered around the bushes, avoiding the two strange figures . . . As the days passed the trust deepened and we played and had fun together.'[9] A degree of caution was always taken. 'Oliver was very nippy', recalls McKenna, 'so whenever he was nearby you made sure you tucked your fingers in because he was rather apt to nibble them.'[10] On screen, finger-nibbling was not a problem. The chemistry between Merrill, the character based on Gavin Maxwell, and Mij captivated audiences. This reflected the off-screen relationship between Travers and Dusky. During an interview with the *Telegraph Magazine* McKenna explained that this rapport developed with time: 'Gradually he started to look at us a bit less suspiciously. Then, one day, he came up to us. He sniffed my husband's boots. Then he started crawling over his legs. Those two ended up getting on so well; Dusky would just follow him everywhere.'[11]

The film adaptation was loosely based on Gavin Maxwell's novel. The screenplay, co-written by Couffer and Travers, was quite unlike the original. Aspects of Maxwell's life were disregarded,

Mary MacKenzie, played by Virginia McKenna, with Johnnie and Mij. Movie still from *Ring of Bright Water*, 1969.

the story changed, and individuals transformed into fictional characters. The lead character, Graham Merrill (Travers), is an insurance agent disillusioned with life in London. While walking home from work an otter catches his eye in a pet-shop window. From this first encounter Merrill believes the otter has singled him out from the thousands of passers-by. Flattered at being 'the chosen one', he buys the animal and names him Mij. The inquisitive pet proves too much for a small apartment. Merrill decides to escape the confines of the city. The unlikely couple set off for a new idyllic life in the Scottish Highlands. A single-roomed croft in an isolated bay becomes their home. A self-sufficient lifestyle is adopted. Beachcombing, fishing and shark hunting become the norm. Merrill befriends the local village doctor, Mary MacKenzie (McKenna). This added love interest sees the three become inseparable. Their lives revolve around Mij.

The film firmly challenges traditional ideas about the otter. The audience is urged to question their own understanding of the animal throughout. The moral distinction between wild and tame becomes increasingly blurred. When Merrill travels with Mij by train, for instance, he decides to buy a dog ticket. When asked what kind of dog it is, Merrill replies: 'A diving terrier.' The assumed relationship between different animal species is also considered. When Mij and Jonnie first meet, Merrill and MacKenzie have a thought-provoking conversation. 'I've always heard that dogs and otters are deadly enemies', claims the doctor. 'Yes, but Mij doesn't know he's an otter', insists Merrill. 'How funny', replies MacKenzie, 'Johnny doesn't know he's a dog.' This important scene shows viewers that the idea of animal identity is a human concept. The dog is not a natural enemy of the otter. It has been trained to be so. The otter is not the natural enemy of people, but has only been labelled as such. There are reminders that this is not a generally accepted idea. A scene in the village post office shows two locals gossiping about Merrill and Mij. The customer says: 'I've nothing against folk fraternizing with animals, but an otter, oh, there's something very strange about that if you ask me.' 'Oh, very strange indeed,' agrees the shopkeeper while stroking her pet cat.

At the end of the film Merrill travels back to London, leaving Mij with MacKenzie. Tragedy then strikes. Angus, the road mender, indiscriminately kills Mij with a spade. The murder of Mij is unexpected. Some may even argue it spoils a perfectly happy story. Indeed, after ninety minutes of warm-hearted family entertainment it does seem out of place. By this time the audience has grown close to Mij. For him to be violently killed is quite the emotional wrench. But that was the aim. The death was based on reality. The real Mij was killed in the same way by a man called Angus. The scene demonstrated the mainstream view of the animal. 'I thought it was just an otter!' Angus insists. The otter was killed as its reputation preceded it. For Gavin Maxwell, the scene was definitely 'far too near the bone'.[12] Judging from the horrified gasps in cinemas, one would assume audiences also felt the otter was worth more than just a spade to the skull.

The film was a commercial success. Gavin Maxwell particularly enjoyed the adaptation. In 1969 he wrote to Travers and McKenna, thanking them for their involvement. The card read:

> Hands too cold to write at length, but this is just to tell you that Jack Couffer showed me *Ring of Bright Water* last week, and I thought it nothing short of magnificent. What splendid performances you both made, and I think I'm one of the comparatively few people who can appreciate just how difficult it must have been. It was very strange to see on the screen a chunk of one's own life apparently being lived by someone else – but it was so well done that it really seemed like that.[13]

A remarkable turn of events considering Maxwell had dismissed the script as a 'sham, a prostitution' and 'a crime'[14] when he first read it.

Ring of Bright Water undoubtedly endeared the otter to a new generation of film fans. It also renewed broader interests in bringing another literary otter to life. In 1971 the possibility of adapting *Tarka* into a film was raised by British film and television producer David Cobham. Cobham was noted for making wildlife documentaries for the BBC. The prospect of a faithful adaptation excited Williamson. He accepted the film proposal and got to work on a script. The thought of writing a treatment for the film did not, however, fill him with joy: 'I dread the idea of the job. At the same time I must have something to do – yet I am so tired, indeed sick of, H.W. as author.'[15] Two years later the 'Tarka treatment' had grown to 180,000 words in length and incorporated another two novels. Sadly, old age, ill health and the onset of dementia had proved too much for Williamson. He passed on responsibility for the screenplay to Cobham and the respected conservationist Gerald Durrell. *Tarka* reached

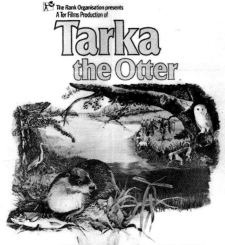

The Rank Organisation presents
A Tor Films Production of

Tarka
the Otter

From the novel by HENRY WILLIAMSON · Screenplay by GERALD DURRELL and DAVID COBHAM · Story Teller PETER USTINOV
Music Composed by DAVID FANSHAWE
Produced and Directed by DAVID COBHAM
Photography TERRY CHANNELL and JOHN McCALLUM
Underwater Photography SLIM MacDONNELL · Edited by CHARLES DAVIES
Associate Producers FRANCIS POWIS and JANET COBHAM

Poster promoting the cinema release of *Tarka the Otter* in 1979.

Behind the scenes shot of *Tarka the Otter*.

the big screen in 1979. The audience was guided by the voice of revered British actor Peter Ustinov, who had been cast as the story-teller. The cinematography and narration helped turn Tarka into an iconic filmic star. The natural performance mesmerized viewers, as it still does today. People could be forgiven for thinking they are watching footage of a wild animal.

The filming, which started in 1976, took over two years to complete. Each scene demanded meticulous planning and preparation. Cobham went to great lengths to create an authentic experience. The majority of filming, for instance, took place in and around the River Torridge in Devon. When they found that the Owlery Holt tree had disappeared, a fibre-glass replica took its place on the riverbank. The role of Tarka was played by two tame otters. The first was Spade. This young otter had been hand-reared by Jeanne Wayre, a co-founder of the Otter Trust. He also had a special handler, Peter Talbot. After just six months Spade 'would walk to heel just like a dog and come when called'.[16] This meant the Tarka scenes could be shot with relative ease. Spade would be positioned, the cameraman would shout action, and the handler would call for the tame otter. Some scenes were slightly trickier. For these, there was only one solution. 'If we wanted the otter to stop at a particular rock in the river as if he was following another otter,' David Cobham explained, 'then we'd anoint the rock with fish juice, an irresistible lure.'[17]

The hunting scenes, of course, were a different matter. As the welfare of the otter was of the utmost importance, hounds did not cross paths with a single otter. In fact, the animals did not even share a shot. The picturesque otterhounds in the film came from the Kendal and District OH. A number of techniques were used to make the scenes look as realistic as possible. When Tarka was chased by the hounds, for instance, a trail of scent was made from the tame otter's bedding. The pack would then follow that line when the camera was rolling. Spade could then be encouraged to repeat the process safely once the pack had returned to the Lake District. The famous scene where Deadlock violently lunges at Tarka inside Owlery Holt was also achieved this way. Initially this proved rather troublesome, as the hound cast as Deadlock was calm, even docile. Although the animal bore a striking visual resemblance, he did not have the same aggressive tendencies as the character. Fortunately, like all other dogs, he did have a ferocious appetite for dog food. The crew soon found that 'a tin of "Chum" strategically placed at the back of the holt would ensure an energetic response.'[18]

The final scene in the 'Last Hunt', where Tarka and Deadlock fight to the death, is one of the most memorable in the film. This did not require quite as much energy from Deadlock. The lifeless hound which floats to the surface was actually already dead, having died of natural causes, been frozen, thawed and then prepared with make-up. This meticulous planning made the scene all the more convincing. This part of the film also has added significance. Just hours after it had been shot, the author, Henry Williamson, passed away. Anne Williamson reflected on this in *Tarka and the Last Romantic*: 'It really does seem to have been a most extraordinary point of fate, that it should have happened on the very day that the film crew were filming that particular scene: Henry and Tarka went out together on the ebb tide of the "sea-going waters" of life.'[19]

Returning to the film, a second otter played young Tarka. As otter cubs were extremely hard to come by this part of the filming was left until last. With little hope of finding a cub and a tight deadline to keep, things got desperate. The director even considered using a mink for the role. Fortunately, just before they gave up Cobham got a phone call from Grahame Dangerfield: 'I've got your baby . . . She's about three months old and she's called Pott.'[20] Pott had been injured by a fox terrier on the Isle of

Tarka running from hounds. Movie still from *Tarka the Otter*, 1979.

Young Tarka,
played by Tarkina,
walking along
branch. Movie
still from *Tarka
the Otter*, 1979.

Skye. Dangerfield, the founder of the Wildlife Breeding Centre
in Hertfordshire, received the wounded cub from the dog's
owner and nursed her back to health. On set, Pott was soon
renamed Tarkina. The story of a pitter-patter-pottering otter
called Pott was not quite the handle the press had in mind.

Tarkina starred in three key scenes, two involving water.
Dangerfield was very protective of the cub, and at times reluc-
tant to make the animal perform. He feared the youngster 'might
catch a fatal chill if she spent too much time in the water'.[21]
Extreme measures were taken to ensure this did not happen. The
day of filming in Hampshire at a specially constructed water
tank is a prime example. Tarkina had to be dropped from above
the tank and filmed as she plunged underwater. As it was a cold
day with poor natural lighting the scene had to be repeated until
perfect. Dangerfield came fully equipped with hot water bottles,
towels and a constantly running car heater. The young otter
received the highest level of care: 'In between each plunge into
the river Grahame rushed Tarkina back to the car, where the

Emmet Otter performing with the Frogtown Jubilee Jug-Band.

temperature had reached jungle heat, and rubbed her down until she was warm and dry and ready for her next dip into the icy water.'[22] It is perhaps no surprise that Tarkina finished the day unscathed. The young cub soon became a minor celebrity in her own right and made a number of children's television appearances in the UK. After appearing on Jonny Morris's TV show *Animal Magic*, there were similar items on Noel Edmonds' *Multi-Coloured Swap Shop*, *Blue Peter* and *Clapperboard*.[23]

Jim Henson, the creator of *Sesame Street* and the *Muppet Show*, was also drawn to the otter. He identified Russell Hoban's children's book *Emmet Otter's Jug-Band Christmas* as an ideal story for adaptation. Emmet and his Ma live along the river near Frogtown Hollow. Having little money, they expect another bleak Christmas. When they hear the local talent contest has a $50 prize they both secretly enter. There they face stiff competition from the Riverbottom Nightmare Band. Henson adapted the story into a one-hour television special for HBO in 1977. Three years later it was broadcast by ABC in the United States. With its catchy songs and happy ending, the special became a family favourite.[24] Repeated broadcasts on prime-time television meant millions of North American viewers fell in love with this version of the animal.[25]

Over the past twenty years wild otters have appeared on our screens on a more regular basis. Wildlife documentaries filmed in natural environments have undoubtedly maintained public interest in the animal.[26] Yet the on-screen otter still escaped the attention of certain viewers. Its profile was raised by a rather unlikely fictional source: J. K. Rowling's *Harry Potter*. Each character has a Patronus charm, a protector in animal form. Harry himself has a stag, his friend Ron Weasley a Jack Russell terrier, and Hermione Granger has an otter. This animated scene first appeared on our screens in the film adaptation of *Harry Potter and the Order of the Phoenix* in 2007. Although the appearance is only brief, the animal reached an unprecedented audience. The film grossed $938.2 million at the global box office. If this did not improve the popularity of the animal, the opinion of the author did. A common talking point among Harry Potter fans was Animagus, the ability to morph into an animal. The question 'which animal would you be?' had been posed since the first book was published in 1997. When J. K. Rowling was asked, the author had an interesting answer: 'I'd like to be an otter – that's my favourite animal.'[27]

7 Protecting the Otter

Across the world otters have been persecuted for centuries, valued for their fur and flesh, and killed for profit, pleasure, fashion and revenge. With this troubled history it is quite remarkable they have survived into the twenty-first century. Today the remaining species are largely protected by national laws and international cooperation.[1] Despite this there is still a downward population trend, with all 13 species appearing on the IUCN (2008) *Red List for Threatened Species* (see appendix, table 2). Five are categorized as endangered (hairy-nosed, marine, southern river, giant and sea); two as vulnerable (Asian small-clawed and smooth-coated), and one as near threatened (Eurasian). Not one of the assessed species boasts a growing population. This raises a number of important questions. Why are otters not flourishing in the wild? What has put them under so much pressure? Can they be saved from extinction? And what can be done to improve their hopes of survival? The predicament of each species is, of course, unique. As this book has shown, the animal's identity has been formed by different cultures and traditions. There are, however, a wide range of shared threats.

The age-old reputation of otter as fish-killer is a universal problem. Not everyone subscribes to the cute and cuddly image made popular by the literary and onscreen otter. In areas where fishing is important the animal is regarded as a destructive nuisance. In

Sir Harry Johnston called for the legal protection of Eurasian otters. He argued they were 'far more beautiful, wonderful, and "obvious" than any fish'. Coloured plate by Sir Harry Johnston, from *British Mammals*, 1903.

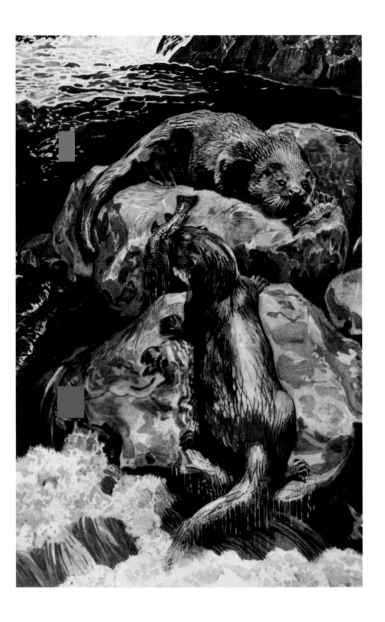

East African lakes, for instance, spotted-necked otters remove about 10 per cent of fish from the nets of local fishermen.[2] Aquaculture projects in south Asia also regularly lose fish and shrimps to both small-clawed and smooth-coated otters.[3] In Europe the angling fraternity regularly blames Eurasian otters for wiping out fish stocks. Despite being an emblem of wildlife conservation in the UK, there have been controversial calls for a cull. One such advocate stated: 'Fisheries are being absolutely destroyed by these cuddly, little murdering blighters . . . No one wants widespread mass slaughter, but there is a need for very targeted culling.'[4] Richard Lee, editor of the *Angling Times*, also made a frank admission in 2009: 'The slaughter of these animals has been driven underground. It is already going on. If you watch £20,000 worth of stock disappear in just a few days, what are the owners going to do?'[5] This covert killing is happening on a global scale.

Another contributing factor to the continued plight of otters is the commercial value of their skins. Although CITES has outlawed the import and export of protected species, there is still a market for otter fur. An astonishing number of animals are slaughtered for this illegal trade. In 1977, for example, a massive haul of skins including 15,470 neotropical and 271 giant otters were intercepted entering the US. Remarkably, this was the spoils of just one New York dealer.[6] The source of these skins, South America, was still providing illegal pelts in the 1990s. In southern Chile the marine otter was singled out by fishermen. With a pelt worth the equivalent of three months wages, and little chance of being fined, it is easy to see why this remains a prevalent practice.[7] It has been estimated that there are now fewer than 1,000 marine otters left in the wild.

Recent figures from the International Otter Survival Fund (IOSF, established in 1993) suggest that Asia has an even more widespread problem, with the main culprits being identified as India and China. In October 2003 778 otter skins were seized at Sangsang, Tibet. Two years later India's most wanted wildlife product smuggler, Sansar Chand, was reported to have supplied between 3,275 and 3,825 otter skins to eight different Nepalese and Tibetan buyers. In 2006 1,833 skins were found openly on sale in Linxiain Gansu Province, China.[8] One reason for this exploitation is tradition. As otter fur is used in Tibetan national dress it is in high demand. The *Times of India News Network* reported on the chupa in 2005: 'They were everywhere. In upscale shops in old Lhasa, on the streets of Linxiain China's Gansu province and on the bodies of young men and women attending horse festivals in Tibet. But there's one image – a young man wearing a traditional Tibetan dress embellished with six otter heads.'[9]

Alarmed by this relentless slaughter, the IOSF publicized the otter as the 'forgotten animal of the fur trade'. To counter this they launched the Furget-me-not campaign in Cambodia. 'Everyone always thinks about tigers and leopards or elephant ivory, but the trade in otter furs is huge', stated co-founder Paul Yoxon in 2007. 'Most otters are captured by fishermen who are very poor and simply seek to earn additional money. By engaging these fishermen into the research and conservation of the otters instead of shunning them . . . we can give these people an otter-friendly alternative to their destructive activities and provide real protection for the otters.'[10]

This educational approach is slowly changing attitudes of those directly involved. It has been strengthened by the public exhibition of Dara, the world's only captive hairy-nosed otter. The species was believed to be extinct as recently as 1998, but has since been discovered in Cambodia, Vietnam, Thailand and Sumatra. Today fewer than 300 individuals remain in the wild,

Buddhist monks bless Dara and his new home.

and from summer 2008 Dara remained single at Phnom Tamau Zoological Garden and Rescue Centre to his death in 2010. As well as becoming a popular attraction, his presence made a more significant impact: 'The Cambodian people are seeing Dara and now don't want to kill otters. Dara has become the real "star of hope" for otters in Cambodia and south east Asia.'[11] If public perceptions can change then otters will have a better chance of survival. If a couple can be found, captive breeding may also prove a useful method for protecting this endangered species.

Intentional lutracide is not the only threat. As 'otters inhabit often fragile ecosystems with both aquatic and terrestrial characteristics',[12] they are vulnerable to broader human activities. The draining of wetlands, construction of dams, use of aquaculture technologies, removal of bank side vegetation, and canalization of rivers all lead to habitat destruction. Fishing nets, boat propellers and road vehicles each indiscriminately take lives. The disappearance of forests, changing agricultural practices and sewage are also responsible for waterways becoming contaminated by chemical and biological pollutants. The conservation of the giant otter is a fine example, as the species will not survive without habitat protection. Nicole Duplaix underlined this point in her 2002 World Wildlife Fund report:

Otter mortality on roads is a common problem. One preventative measure is the use of road signs such as this photographed in the Outer Hebrides.

> The three Guianas remain the last stronghold of Giant otters in South America, with pristine Giant otter habitat on some rivers and good Giant otter densities overall – still, but for how long? The survival of the Giant otter populations in the Guianas is essential to the survival of this endangered species in South America.[13]

As the only hairy-nosed otter in captivity Dara helped improve the public reputation of otters in Cambodia.

Oil spills are another major danger. There was a catastrophic incident in March 1989, when the *Exxon Valdez* struck a reef causing 41 million litres of crude oil to spill into the Prince William Sound, Alaska. This disaster killed millions of marine organisms, including between 750 and 2,800 sea otters. This figure would have been much higher had it not been for the sea otter rescue mission, which cost US$18.2 million.[14] The long term ecological impacts of this terrible incident are still being felt today.

Sea otters are an excellent example of a keystone predator and sentinel species. Their presence is essential for maintaining a healthy coastal environment and their plight acts as a useful indicator of human hazards. Their revival has been a major success story, yet the possibility of extinction is still very real. If a

Giant otters will only survive in the wild if their habitat is protected.

One of the many
sea otters killed by
the *Exxon Valdez*
oil spill in March
1989.

single event like *Exxon* was to happen in California it would potentially wipe out the whole southern sea otter population.[15]

A more pervasive threat is from parasites and disease. In 2003 a detailed study of otter carcasses on the Californian coast found that 63.8 per cent died from disease.[16] Surprisingly, the most prominent parasite found was *Toxoplasma gondii*, usually common in cats. It is thought that infected cat faeces is being washed into the ocean and ingested by otters. Animal loving cat owners are indirectly contributing to the deaths of an endangered species. New laws have been introduced to help reduce

An oiled Californian sea otter, named Olive, recuperates after cleaning. After six weeks of rehabilitation she was released into the wild.

this threat. Since 2006 all cat litter sold in California must carry a warning label advising customers not to throw their pet's waste into storm drains or toilets. A $25,000 penalty was also introduced to discourage any direct harm to the animal. More recently the Southern Sea Otter Recovery and Research Act (2009) has ensured that funding is provided to address current threats.

In Alaska northern sea otters are also losing their lives, but to a very different killer. Natural predation by killer whales was almost unheard of until the early 1990s, when the northern population declined dramatically. It was discovered that areas accessed by killer whales lost 76 per cent of its sea otters within five years, whereas those without them continued to maintain stable populations. When researchers calculated the food requirements of killer whales it was estimated that 'only 3.7 of these animals would need to change feeding habits for them to consume 40,000 sea otters'.[17] These figures are alarming, but they are only projections and may not become a reality. In this case scientific uncertainty is reassuring. Nevertheless, if conservationists can continue raising public awareness, improving coastal habitats and protecting the species, populations should naturally increase.

The perfect example of otter protection comes from the UK, where the Eurasian otter was once on the cusp of extinction. In the twentieth century the public image of the animal underwent a complete reversal: 'Once regarded as a voracious predatory vermin, otters are now seen by most people as attractive and interesting.'[18] When *BBC Wildlife* magazine conducted a poll for Britain's favourite mammal in 2008, the otter came in at number one. It isn't just its popularity that has improved; the species is now thriving. Many lessons can be learnt from this turnaround. In fact, it should be viewed as a useful survival guide for the species. So what led to these changes?

Knowledge about the otter still came from hunting experience in the mid-twentieth century. As Watkins et al. noted in

Sea otters are threatened by pollution, disease and natural predation.

2007: 'the otter is not an animal the scientists and scientific organisations could confidently claim to know'.[19] Political attempts to protect it were invariably opposed to the practice. The LACS introduced the Protection of Animals (Hunting and Coursing Prohibition) Bill in 1949. Although it failed to become legislation, it led to the appointment of the Home Office Committee on Cruelty to Wild Animals. The eight-person committee included Scott Henderson and Frances Pitt, and their report was published in 1951. It found that otters were largely out of sight, but 'well distributed on most of the waterways, pools and lakes of Great Britain'. It also stated 'they are regarded as scarcer than is in fact the case', due to their 'retiring and secretive' ways.[20] The report acknowledged: 'Hunting does undoubtedly involve suffering for the otter, and the degree of it is rather greater than in most other field sports.' It also questioned 'If the otter population has to be controlled', and recommended that 'a thorough investigation should be conducted . . . into the natural history of the otter.'[21]

As a result of this recommendation The Otter Committee was formed in 1951. Their research was commissioned by the Nature Conservancy, and supported by the Universities Federation for Animal Welfare (UFAW). Investigator Marie Stephens studied the animal from 1952 to 1954, combining hunting knowledge with scientific observations. When *The Otter Report* was published in 1958, Stephens admitted: 'Although far more numerous in the British Isles than is generally realised, otters are rather sparsely distributed.'[22]

The Otter Report roused the interest of naturalists. The UFAW was eager to continue researching the animal but lacked funding. When Charles Hume approached the Nature Conservancy, the Director General gave a rather insightful response:

> While we would . . . always be ready to consider a fresh
> application for renewed research on this interesting
> beast, it was our impression that lack of co-operation by
> otters was . . . a difficulty . . . and that it would probably
> be more profitable to concentrate for the time being on
> more easily studied predators such as the Pine Marten
> and the Fox.[23]

For Max Nicholson the otter was not a chief concern, it was
difficult to find and expensive to study. Animals with greater
visibility were more co-operative and therefore higher up the
research agenda.

The first indication that otters may be in danger came from
the hunting fraternity. In 1962 an article titled, 'Where are the
Otters?' appeared in *Gamekeeper and Countryside*. The author,
Jack Ivestor Lloyd, drew attention to the increasingly unseen
status of the animal: 'until two or three seasons ago, plenty *were*
found. But not now . . . What has happened to the otters?'[24] A
number of suggestions were made for the perceived decline,
including pollution, trapping, tourism, river clearance, dredg-
ing and a shortage of frogs. Lloyd was confident hunting was
not to blame: 'Of one thing I am certain, that of all the many
threats to an otter's survival, that of the hunter and his hounds
is the least.'[25] The concern for the otter was such that all hunts
adopted a voluntary restriction on killing from 1964. This concern revived interest from the scientific community. In 1968 the
Mammal Society was commissioned to investigate the status of
the animal and their results confirmed the underlying fears.
The report stated: 'There appears no doubt that, over the southern part of Great Britain there has been a very considerable
decrease in the otter population . . . Only in very few localised
areas are there any indications of a stable population or of an

increasing one.'[26] Hunting was not blamed, but the following recommendations were made: 'For at least the next five to ten years . . . the killing of otters and further pollution should be reduced as much as possible.'[27]

The declining otter soon became the subject of political debate. On 13 May 1969 Edwin Brooks introduced the Protection of Otters Bill. Brooks had a sentimental view of the animal which was largely informed by the literary otter: 'Williamson's classic gave me a lasting affection for the animal which Gavin Maxwell's more recent *Ring of Bright Water* has confirmed. It is hard not to see our better human qualities in the otter's great sense of play, and in the exemplary maternal instincts of the female.'[28] Although Brooks primarily targeted 'killing for pleasure or pelt', the possibility of extinction was central to his argument. 'The object of the Bill is simply to conserve a wild creature of our countryside',[29] he insisted. The following day the Bill roused media interest. Headlines such as 'MP Campaigns to Save Otters from Extinction' and 'One MP could Kill the Bill to Save Otters', appeared in the *Guardian* and *Morning Post*.

The Bill did not reach second reading. It was, however, re-introduced by Ray Carter in February 1972. On this occasion there was a growing sense of urgency. The otter had been added to the 'list of animals in greatest danger of extinction'[30] by organisations such as the World Wildlife Trust. Carter was afraid this could be the last chance to save the species: 'Two years have elapsed since the last attempt was made to classify the otter as a protected animal. Should this attempt fail, it is conceivable that the need for a third will have been removed, the otter having disappeared from rural and water life.'[31] Despite the looming inevitability this attempt also failed to reach legislation.

Nevertheless, new otter protection groups emerged. Philip Wayre and Jeanne Perkins (who married in 1975) founded the

Postcard of Jeanne Wayre holding Eurasian otter cubs. The Otter Trust were pioneers of captive breeding and reintroducing British Eurasian otters into the wild.

Otter Trust in 1971. Wayre recalls: 'They were threatened with extinction, which very few other things were. I think that was the thing. It became obvious that unless we did something about them they were going to disappear.'[32] To counter this, four objectives were set. First, to promote the conservation of otters throughout the world wherever it was necessary for their survival. Second, to maintain a collection of otters in semi-natural but controlled conditions, for research, public interest and education. Third, to carry out research into the breeding of otters in captivity, with the ultimate aim of releasing young animals wherever suitable habitat remained. Fourth, to promote and support field studies of otters in order to collect factual scientific information to help in their management and conservation.[33] In 1975 they purchased River Farm, a twenty-six acre site in Earsham, Suffolk, and added twenty-one large breeding enclosures to the existing lake, river and marshes. Thirteen pens were swiftly occupied by British, Indian smooth-coated and Asian short-clawed otters. When the centre opened to the public in 1976, admission fees were charged to support the breeding programme, with annual visitors exceeding 40,000. Another new organization, the Otter Specialist Group, was formed in 1974 as part of the World Conservation (IUCN) Species Survival Commission (SSC), and Friends of the Earth also started a campaign to 'Save the Otter'.

There was further evidence of the otter's decline in 1974 when the Mammal Society published their second report. Although it suggested that otters had 'held their own or increased slightly' in some counties, it stressed that 'in the Midlands especially the decline continues, and the otter can truthfully be described as a locally endangered species'.[34] This was reinforced by two independent surveys carried out in Suffolk and Norfolk.[35] These surveys excluded hunting records, instead relying on the observations of naturalists. All indications of otter presence, including signs, spraints, footprints and food remains, were mapped. The results suggested that there were 34 otters in Norfolk and 36 in Suffolk, considerably fewer than expected for East Anglia. This mounting concern saw the creation of the Joint Otter Group in September 1976, made up of specialists from the Institute of Terrestrial Ecology, the Mammal Society, the Nature Conservancy Council, the Otter Haven Project, and the Society for the Promotion of Nature Conservation. The group's first report, *Otters, 1977*, concluded there had been a 'downward trend', and that there was 'no suggestion of any improvement'.[36]

The anti blood-sports movement had also continued to raise public awareness. Thirty thousand people joined the League

Against Cruel Sports letter-writing campaign and 248 MPs signed a motion urging for the otter's legal protection. Amendments to the existing legislation ensured the otter became a protected species in England and Wales. From 1 January 1978 it became illegal to kill, injure, take, or attempt to do any of these things to an otter. With this, otter hunting ended in Britain.[37] New scientific evidence from Paul Chanin and Don Jefferies published in 1978 identified toxic chemicals as the main cause of the otter population collapse. They argued it coincided with broader animal decline: 'huge wildlife casualties were a feature of the English countryside from 1956 to 1961 when the organochlorine insecticides, dieldrin, aldrin and heptachlor were used as cereal and seed dressings.'[38] The use of dieldrin, which was specifically singled out, had been largely banned by 1966.

From 1982 this protection extended to Scotland under the Wildlife and Countryside Act. This national act included habitat

The League Against Cruel Sports helped raise public awareness of the declining otter population in Britain in the 1960s and '70s.

A child protesting against the sport.

protection, and the destruction or disturbance of dens belonging to protected animals became an offence. Soon after these provisions the Otter Trust started to reintroduce otters back to the wild. In June 1983 two females and an unrelated male were released in an uninhabited river in Suffolk. Harnesses and radio transmitters were secured to track their movements. This trial proved to be a success. As Wayre explains in *Operation Otter,* the released animals not only survived, they established territories and behaved like wild otters.[39] After just a year it was discovered that one of the females had also given birth. The next release generated more publicity, with television coverage on the BBC series *Q.E.D.* As public interest in the animal grew, so did the Otter Trust. Two additional havens were set up. The Tamar Otter Park opened near Launceston, Cornwall, in 1986, and ten years later this was joined by the North Pennines Reserve near Bowes, County Durham.

The breeding and reintroduction programme continued to go from strength to strength. By 1999 117 otters had been released to the wild. This was such a success that the Trust chose

In the twenty-first century Eurasian otters thrive in Britain.

to close the Earsham Centre to the public from October 2006. British otters no longer needed to be bred in captivity, as approximately 10,395 were now thriving in the wild.[40] After 35 years of otter conservation Philip Wayre could proudly announce: 'mission accomplished'. With this he received national recognition, and quite rightly so, described in the *Telegraph* as 'the man who saved Britain's otters'.[41] Just months later, conservationists announced a nationwide return of the species: 'More than 40 years after dangerous agricultural chemicals almost wiped otters off the map of England, our most charismatic mammal is finally back in every county.'[42]

Today otters throughout the world are in desperate need of protection. The phenomenal achievement of saving species from the brink of extinction in Britain and North America very much paves the way for the rest of the world to follow. With education, scientific study and public support, the otter can escape its image of persecuted, endangered victim and emerge as a proud and enduring symbol of survival.

Appendix: Otter Data

TABLE 1. FAMILY TREE OF OTTERS

Species and genera of the subfamily Lutrinae, with approximate age of separation in millions of years

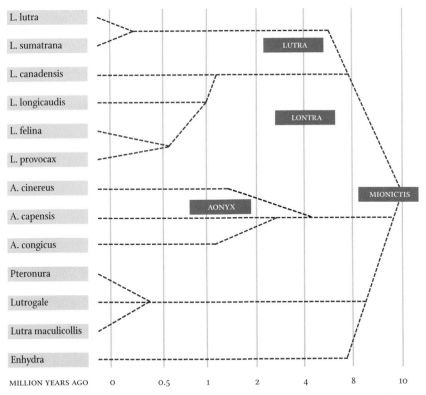

Source: H. Kruuk, 2006, p. 31 Based on data from Koepfli and Wayne (1998) and Bininda-Emonds et al. (1999)

TABLE 2. THREATENED SPECIES

Otter	Species Authority	Category	Population Trend
Hairy-nosed *Lutra sumatrana*	Gray 1865	Endangered	Decreasing <300
Marine *Lontra feline*	Molina 1782	Endangered	Decreasing <1,000
Southern river *Lontra provacax*	Thomas 1908	Endangered	Decreasing
Giant *Pteronura brasiliensis*	Gmelin 1788	Endangered	Decreasing 1,000-5,000
Sea *Enhydra lutris* – Northern – Southern – Russian	Linnaeus 1758	Endangered	Stable 64,600–77,300 2,800 15,000
Asian small-clawed *Aonyx cinerea*	Illiger 1815	Vulnerable	Decreasing
Smooth-coated *Lutrogale perspicilata*	Saint-Hilaire 1826	Vulnerable	Unknown
Eurasian *Lutra lutra*	Linnaeus 1758	Near Threatened	Decreasing
Cape clawless *Aonyx capensis*	Schinz 1821	Least Concern	Stable
Spotted-necked *Lutra maculicollis*	Lichtenstein 1835	Least Concern	Decreasing
Congo clawless *Aonyx congica*	Lönnberg 1910	Least Concern	Unknown
North American *Lontra Canadensis*	Schreber 1777	Least Concern	Stable
Neotropical *Lontra longicaudis*	Olfers 1818	Data Deficient	Decreasing

Source: D. Allen, 2010, after IUCN Red List (2008)

TABLE 3. ECOLOGY AND BEHAVIOUR

Otter Species	Distribution	Gestation (Delayed Implantation*)	Litter	Weight (kg)	Length (m)	Diurnal/ Nocturnal	Solitary / Group	Life expectancy (captive, c)
Eurasian	Eur/Asia/Africa	60–63	2–3	7–10	1–1.3	N–D	S	22c
N. American	N. America	60–63*	1–5	8–9	1.25	D–N	S/G	23c
Giant	S. America	65–70	1–3	22–34	2	D	G	12c
Neotropical	Ibid.	56	2–3	12	1.2	D	S	?
Southern river	Ibid.	63	1–2	7–11	1–1.3	N	S	10
Marine	Ibid.	60–65	2–5	3–6	0.9	D	S/G	?
Hairy-nosed	Asia	?	?	7–8	1–1.3	D–N	S	?
Smooth-coated	Ibid.	63–65	2–4	9–11	1.1–1.3	D-N	G	20c
Small-clawed	Ibid.	62	2–7	3.5	0.8	D	G	11c
Cape clawless	Africa	63	2–3	18	1.8	N–D	S/G	11c
Congo clawless	Ibid.	?	?	25	1.5	?	S	?
Spotted-necked	Ibid.	63	1–3	3–6	1	D–N	G	20c
Sea	N. Am / Asia	65–70*	1	20–45	1.2–1.6	D	S/G	19–23

Source: D. Allen, 2010, after H. Kruuk (2006), IUCN Red List (2008), IOSF (2009), and WAZA (2009)

Timeline of the Otter

20 million BC	10 million BC	1500 BC	1000 BC
The earliest recognized otter genus, *Mionictis*, dates back to the early Miocene	Evolutionary divergence of otter species begins	Archaeological remains prove that indigenous peoples of the Pacific Northwest hunted sea otters for their fur, flesh, bones and teeth. It is not known when this practice first started, probably many centuries before	Remains of burnt sea otter bones found in Californian middens. In southern Sweden petroglyphs were found in a burial site in Kivik, featuring stylized animals which appear to represent captive otters 

1566	1742	1745–1822	1906
In England the otter is classified as vermin under the 'Acte for the Preservation of Grayne' 	After months of being shipwrecked on Bering Island, naturalist Georg Steller and other survivors return to Russia with hundreds of sea otter pelts	Over 750,000 sea otter skins are sold in the international fur trade 	The RSPCA agrees to prepare a bill to make otter hunting illegal in Britain, but rescind their decision two months later

1971	1975	1978	1989
Philip Wayre and Jeanne Perkins set up the Otter Trust in the UK, the world's first otter conservation organization	The Convention on International Trade in Endangered Species of Wild Fauna and Flora (CITES) is agreed: all otters are listed	The otter becomes a protected species in England and Wales. It becomes illegal to kill, injure or take them. This law is extended to Scotland in 1982	The *Exxon Valdez* oil spill kills millions of marine organisms, including between 750 and 2,800 sea otters

<400	721	1157	1323–8

The otter is sacred the Zoroastrian people of ancient Persia. The animal appears in the *Avesta Vandidad*

Life and Miracles of St Cuthbert published, the story of the Northumbrian monk and the otters was recounted

The first institutional pack of otter hounds is formed in England when Henry II appoints a King's Otterer

Friar Odoric observes otter fishing, or fishing with otters, on the Yangtze River, south-west China. This practice has been traced back to AD 600

11	1927	1939	1969

The commercial hunting of sea otters ends when the United States, Russia, Great Britain and Japan agree the Fur Seal Treaty

Henry Williamson's *Tarka the Otter* published. The following year the book won the Hawthornden Prize

Tarka the Otter

Emil E. Liers takes twelve of his trained otters to Manhattan for the Annual National Sportsmen's Show. He later wrote *An Otter's Story* (1953)

Gavin Maxwell's (1960) *Ring of Bright Water* adapted into a film

989	1998	2008	2010

Eurasian otter declared extinct in the Netherlands. A reintroduction scheme starts in 2002

Hairy-nosed otters thought to be extinct, but rediscovered in Thailand the following year

Five otter species listed as endangered on the IUCN's *Red List for Threatened Species*

Dara, the only hairy-nosed otter in captivity, dies of an infection just two years after being released into his public enclosure

References

1 INTRODUCING THE OTTER

1 Philip Wayre, *The River People* (Glasgow, 1977), p. 121.
2 Hans Kruuk, *Otters: Ecology, Behaviour and Conservation* (Oxford, 2006), p. 223.
3 Clement J. Harris, *Otters: A Study of the Recent Lutrinae* (1968), cited in Paul Chanin, *The Natural History of Otters* (London, 1985), p. 4.
4 Chanin in ibid. explains that this was based on vocalizations, the shape of the baculum (penis bone) and the appearance of the male external genitalia.
5 International Union for Conservation of Nature (2008), at www.iucn.org.
6 IUCN Otter Specialist Group (2006), at www.otterspecialistgroup. org.
7 Gilbert White, *The Natural History and Antiquities of Selborne* (London, 1837), p. 138.
8 Delabere Pritchett Blaine, *An Encyclopaedia of Rural Sports* (London, 1840), p. 540.
9 There are regional variations. Coastal-dwelling otters, such as those in Scotland, are diurnal and therefore active during the day. The species is extremely solitary. Any groups tend to be mothers with her cubs, who can stay together for up to 15 months. Breeding occurs throughout the year.
10 In recent years otter experts have maintained that this is exceptional behaviour. If otters are left undisturbed while feeding, very little is left behind. Larger prey is caught and scavenged. This meat can provide several meals before it becomes too rotten.

Nevertheless, such remnants do provide an indication of an otter's former presence. Lesley Wright, pers. comm., 2010.

11 T. Sefass and P. Polechla, 'Lontra canadensis', in *IUCN Red List of Threatened Species* (2008), at www.iucnredlist.org.

12 Kruuk, *Otters*, p. 15.

13 Ibid., p. 13.

14 C. F. Mason and S. M. Macdonald, *Otters: Ecology and Conservation* (Cambridge, 1986), p. 192.

15 Keith and Liz Laidler, *The River Wolf* (London, 1983), p. 1.

16 Ibid.

17 Derek Grzelewski, 'Otter Fascinating,' *Smithsonian Magazine*, November 2002.

18 Kruuk, *Otters*, p. 16.

19 Ibid., p. 17.

20 In the 1930s a small population was also transplanted to the Falkland Islands for their fur. William L. Franklin and Melissa M. Grigione, 'The Enigma of Guanacos in the Falkland Islands: The Legend of John Hamilton', *Journal of Biogeography*, XXXII/4 (2005), pp. 661–75.

21 Although Maxwell's otter is widely regarded as extinct, experts have recently found smooth-coated otters in the Iraqi marshes. Members of the Otter Specialist Group are hopeful that further research will lead to the rediscovery of *Lutrogale perspicillata maxwelli*.

22 Pat Foster-Turley and C. Santiapillai, 'Action plan for Asian Otters', in *Otters: An Action Plan for their Conservation*, Pat Foster-Turley, Shelia Macdonald and Chris Mason (Cambridge, 1990), pp. 52–63.

23 Conservation International, 'World's Only Captive Hairy-nosed Otter Gets New Home,' *Biology Online*, 23 June 2008, at www.biology-online.org.

24 Philip Wayre, *Operation Otter* (London, 1989), p. 93

25 World Association of Zoos and Aquariums (2008), at www.waza.org.

26 Gavin Maxwell's companions, Edal and Teko, were both Cape clawless otters.

27 M. Hoffman, 'Aonyx congicus', in *IUCN Red List of Threatened Species*.

28 Sea Otter Alliance (2009), at www.seaotterresearch.org.

29 Stefani Paine, *The Nature of Sea Otters* (San Francisco, 1993), p. 35.

30 John A. Love, *Sea Otters* (London, 1990).

31 Glenn VanBlaricom, 'Relationships of Sea Otters to Living Marine Resources in California: A New Perspective', in *Proceedings of the Ocean Studies Symposium*, ed. V. Lyle, vol. II, Sacramento (November 1982), cited in Roy Nickerson, *Sea Otters: A Natural History and Guide* (San Francisco, 1989), p. 72.

32 Chanin, *The Natural History of Otters*, p. 57.

33 Kruuk, *Otters*, p. 65.

2 FOLKLORE, FABLES, TRADITION AND THE OTTER

1 Max F. Fuller, *Sacred Books of the East* (Oxford, 1879). Greek historian Herodotus (*c.* 449 BC) claimed that the otter was also sacred to the Egyptians. There is, however, little evidence to substantiate this. An otter is pictured on the tomb relief in the Mastaba of Mereruka, Saqqara, Egypt (2300 BC). All other known depictions are of the ichneumon (Egyptian mongoose), an animal which certainly was sacred. Lesley Wright, pers. comm. 2010.

2 Andrew D. White, 'Animal Symbolism in Ecclesiastical Architecture', *Popular Science Monthly*, December 1896, p. 191.

3 Jenny Schroedel, *The Everything Saints Book: The Inspiring Lives of Martyrs and Miracle* (Newton Abbot, 2007), pp. 82–3.

4 Venerable Bede (721), cited in Gerald Bonner, David Rollason and Clare Stancliffe, *St Cuthbert, his Cult and his Community to AD 1200* (Woodbridge, 1998), p. 72.

5 Thomas Pennant, *British Zoology*, vol. I (Dublin, 1818), p. 145.

6 Carl Etter, *Ainu Folklore: Traditions and Culture of the Vanishing Aborigines of Japan, 1949* (New York, 2004), p. 22. In North America the Oneida tribe had a similar creation story to explain the appearance of the animal. In this tale, human immortality would have been achieved if the otter and beaver boated across a lake in silence. The otter laughed, thus ensuring that humans

were mortal. The beaver, who was also the oarsman, hit the otter in the face with his paddle, leaving the animal with a flat nose.

7 Rev. John Batchelor, *The Ainu and Their Folklore* (London, 1901),

8 This version is based on the story as told by Walter Skeat and F. H. Townsend in *Fables and Folk Tales from an Eastern Forest* (Cambridge, 1901), pp. 9–11.

9 Dawn Elaine Bastian and Judy Mitchell, *Handbook of Native American Mythology* (Santa Barbara, CA, 2004), p. 124; Jennifer Hahn, *Spirited Waters: Soloing South Through the Inside Passage* (Leicester, 2009), pp. 88–9.

10 This idea of shape-shifting is also mentioned in Celtic legend. In the shamanic Welsh story of Taliesin, who the enchantress Ceridwen transformed into an otter to pursue her servant Gwion Bach who had plunged into the river as a salmon. Then, of course, in Norse mythology, the god Loki killed Hreidmar's son, Otr, while in the form of an otter and unwittingly presented the father with his pelt. Mad with grief, Hreidmar tied up the gods and demanded a ransom of enough gold to cover the otter skin.

11 Illinois State Museum, 'Meaning of Midewin' (2003), at www.museum.state.il.us.

12 Christina Pratt, *An Encyclopedia of Shamanism*, vol. II (New York, 2007), p. 425.

13 Plenty Coups and Frank Bird Linderman, *Plenty-coups, Chief of the Crows* (Lincoln, NE, 2002), p. 167.

14 Follo's surname differs in various sources. Some record it as Follus, others as le Fol.

15 John Millais, *The Mammals of Great Britain and Ireland* (1905) cited in Angela King, John Ottaway and Angela Potter, *The Declining Otter: A Guide to its Conservation* (Chaffcombe, 1976), p. 17.

16 Colin Antony Howes, 'The Decline of the Otter in South Yorkshire and Adjacent Areas', *Naturalist*, 101 (1976), pp. 3–12, p. 5. Mr Whitaker allegedly sold his dead otters to fur traders and received up to one guinea per pelt.

17 C. W. Hatfield, *Historical Notices of Doncaster*, vol. I (1866), cited in ibid., p. 5.

18 Isaak Walton, *The Complete Angler: Or Contemplative Man's Recreation* (London, 1896), p. 5.

19 In 1888 the book had reached its hundredth edition. By 1914 the edition published by Cassell & Co. in 1886 had sold around 80,000 copies.

20 This demand is exemplified in the rising number of trout fishing licenses held from their introduction in 1879 through to 1910. In 1879 9,109 anglers were listed: by 1900 there had been a rapid rise to 46,757; this figure had steadily increased to 59,655 by 1910.

21 John Waldman, *100 Weird Ways to Catch Fish* (Mechanicsburg, 2005), pp. 124–5.

22 Otto Gabriel, *Von Brandt's Fish Catching Methods of the World* (Oxford, 2005), p. 33.

23 William Bingley, *Animal Biography, or, Popular Zoology* (London, 1829), p. 167.

24 Reza Lubis, 'First Recent Record of Hairy-Nosed Otter in Sumatra, Indonesia', *IUCN Otter Specialist Group Bulletin*, XVIII/1 (2005), pp. 14–20.

25 Gabrielle Hatfield, *Encyclopedia of Folk Medicine: Old World and New World Traditions* (Santa Barbara, CA, 2003), pp. 257–8. Other folkloric tales from Celtic tradition include the Otter King, a mythical creature accompanied by seven black otters, whose pelt if worn rendered warriors invincible. There is also the Irish legend of the Dobhar-chu from County Leitrim, which was said to be five or six times larger than an otter, with pure white fur, black ear tips and a black cross-like mark on its back.

26 John A. Love, *Sea Otters* (London, 1990).

27 IOSF, *Alarming Trade in Otter Furs* (Isle of Skye, 2008), p. 6.

28 Ajanga Khayeai, 'Kenyan Environmentalists Fight to Save the Otter', *News Voice of America.com*, 30 September 2008. In sub-Saharan Africa there are several tribes that wear the fur of the spotted-necked otter as a wristlet. They believe that by wiping it over their eyes and nose, any infections will be cured. Olga Sheean-Stone, *Otters* (Cambridge, 1991), p. 18.

1 Olga Sheean-Stone, *Otters* (Cambridge, 1991), p. 19.

2 Roy Nickerson, *Sea Otters: A Natural History and Guide* (San Francisco, CA, 1989), p. 28.

3 Dean Littlepage, *Steller's Island: Adventures of a Pioneer Naturalist in Alaska* (Seattle, WA, 2006), p. 129.

4 Ibid., p. 132.

5 James R. Gibson, *Otter Skins, Boston Ships, and China Goods: The Maritime Fur Trade of the Northwest Coast, 1785–1841* (London, 1999), p. 13.

6 Paul Chanin, *The Natural History of Otters* (London, 1985), p. 141.

7 Gibson, *Otter Skins, Boston Ships, and China Goods*, p. 13.

8 Nickerson, *Sea Otters*, p. 30.

9 Harold McCracken, *Hunters of the Stormy Sea* (London, 1957), p. 5.

10 Nickerson, *Sea Otters*, p. 38.

11 Ibid., p. 38.

12 Captain Scammon (1872) cited in Nickerson, *Sea Otters*, p. 38.

13 Alexander Allan, *Hunting the Sea Otter* (London, 1910), p. 57.

14 Gibson, *Otter Skins, Boston Ships, and China Goods*, p. 15.

15 Captain James Cook, *A Voyage to the Pacific Ocean, undertaken by the Command of His Majesty for Making Discoveries in the Northern Hemisphere . . . Performed under the Direction of Captains Cook, Clarke, and Gore, and His Majesty's Ships the Resolution and Discovery in the Years 1776-80*, vol. III (London, 1784), p. 437.

16 Gibson, *Otter Skins, Boston Ships, and China Goods*, p. 28.

17 James Gibson has thoroughly documented the scale of the killing in his excellent book, *Otter Skins, Boston Ships, and China Goods*.

18 Gibson, *Otter Skins, Boston Ships, and China Goods*, pp. 318, 181, 278.

19 Lydia Black, *Russians in Alaska, 1732–1867* (Fairbanks, AK, 2004), p. 199.

20 Ibid., p. 288.

21 Chanin, *The Natural History of Otters*, p. 141.

22 Allan, *Hunting the Sea Otter*, pp. 3–4.

23 Henry W. Elliott, *Our Arctic Province* (New York, 1886), p. 127.

24 Glover Morrill Allen, *Extinct and Vanishing Mammals of the Western Hemisphere* (New York, 1942).

25 Stephani Paine, *The Nature of Sea Otters: A Story of Survival* (Vancouver, 1993), p. 107.

26 A stipulation in these laws allows Alaskan sea otter pelts to be used by indigenous peoples in traditional handicrafts.

27 The North American River Otter is still trapped and killed for its pelt in 29 American states and all but one Canadian province. It is a legal requirement to attach CITES tags to these to prove their source of harvest is legitimate.

28 Defenders of Wildlife, Sea Otter (Washington, 2009), at www.defenders.org.

29 IOSF, *The Alarming Trade in Otter Furs* (Isle of Skye, 2008), p. 2.

30 Cliff Atleo (2009) cited in Larry Pynn, 'Vancouver Island First Nations Band Plans to Kill Sea Otters for their Pelts', *Vancouver Sun*, 20 May 2009.

4 OTTER HUNTING FOR SPORT

1 Dr John Henry Walsh, *British Rural Sports* (London, 1856), p. 169.

2 Ludovic Charles Richard Cameron, *Otters and Otter-Hunting* (London, 1908), p. 35.

3 Walsh, *British Rural Sports*, p. 167.

4 'Plunger', 'Reminiscences of Otter Hunting,' *The Field*, 9 August 1862, p. 137.

5 Geoffrey Pring, *Records of the Culmstock Otterhounds, c. 1790–1957* (Exeter, 1958).

6 F. R. J., 'Otter Hunt Extraordinary on the River Otter,' *The Field*, 1 May 1869, p. 373.

7 'Gelert', *Fore's Guide to the Foxhounds and Staghounds of England; to which are added, the Otter-Hounds and Harriers of Several Counties* (London, 1849), pp. 87–8.

8 William Turnbull, *Recollections of an Otter Hunter* (Farrow-on-Tyne, 1896), p. 32.

9 James Lomax, *Diary of Otter Hunting* (Liverpool, 1892), p. 63.

10 Pring, *Records of the Culmstock Otterhounds*, p. 35.

11 Captain T. W. Sheppard, 'Decadence of Otter Hunting', *The Field*, 20 October 1906, p. 658.

12 David Jardine Bell-Irving, *Tally-Ho: Fifty Years of Sporting Reminiscences* (Dumfries, 1920), p. 120.

13 'Otter-Hunting,' *Illustrated London News*, 27 May 1842.

14 Walter Cheesman and Mildred Cheesman, *Diaries of the Crowhurst Otter Hounds* (n.p., 1904), p. 3.

15 Sir William Beach Thomas, *Hunting England* (London, 1936), p. 46.

16 Douglas Macdonald Hastings, 'Hunting the Otter', *Picture Post*, 22 July 1939, p. 54.

17 L. Wardell, 'Otter-Hunting', in Frances Elizabeth Slaughter, *The Sportswoman's Library*, vol. II (London, 1898), pp. 171–81, p. 173

18 Pring, *Records of the Culmstock Otterhounds*, p. 21.

19 Daniel Allen, '"A Delightful Sport with Peculiar Claims": The Specificities of Otter Hunting, 1850–1939', in *Our Hunting Fathers: Field Sports in England after 1850*, ed. Richard Hoyle (Lancaster, 2007), pp. 143–64.

20 Waddy Wadsworth, *Vive La Chasse: A Celebration of British Field Sports Past and Present* (Kent, 1989), p. 128.

21 Reverend Green, *Collections and Recollections of Natural History and Sport: In the Life of a Country Vicar* (London, 1886), pp. 143–4.

22 Douglas Neale, *Nearly All Hunting* (London, 1950), p. 96.

23 Allen, '"A Delightful Sport with Peculiar Claims"', p. 156.

24 Gerald Lascelles, 'Otter', in *Encyclopaedia of Sport*, ed. Hedley Peek and Frederick Aflalo, vol. I (London, 1897), pp. 564–9, p. 564.

25 Arthur Heinemann, 'Otter Hunting', in *The Sports of the World*, ed. Frederick Aflalo (London, 1903), pp. 344–7, p. 346.

26 Aubyn Trevor-Battye, 'July. Otter Hunting', in *A Year of Sport and Natural History*, ed. Oswald Crawford (London, 1895), pp. 158–63, p. 159.

27 Kathleen Frances Barker, *The Young Entry: Fox-Hunting, Beagling and Otter-hunting for Beginners* (London, 1939), p. 114.

28 Allen, '"A Delightful Sport with Peculiar Claims"', p. 160.

29 J. C. Bristow-Noble, 'Should Otter be Hunted?', *Madame*, 9
    September 1905, p. 515.

30 Geoffrey Hill of Hawkstone killed 544 otters between 1870 and
    1884, and William Collier of Culmstock accounted for 144
    between 1879 and 1884. In the 1932–3 season, the 25 packs in exis-
    tence found 905 otters and killed 459.

31 Cheesman and Cheesman, *Diaries of the Crowhurst Otter Hounds*,
    p. 3.

32 Geoffrey R. Mott, *Records of the Dartmoor Otter Hounds, 1740–1940*
    (Dartmoor, 1970), p. 6.

33 Jack Ivester Lloyd, *Come Hunting!* (London, 1952), p. 221.

34 Ernest Bell, 'The Barnstaple Cat-Worrying Case', *The Animals'
    Friend* (1906), p. 43.

35 Ernest Bell, 'Cat Worrying by "Sportsmen"', *The Animals' Friend*
    (1905), pp. 182–3.

36 Bell, 'The Barnstaple Cat-Worrying Case', p. 43.

37 Bell, 'Cat Worrying by "Sportsmen"', pp. 182–3.

38 RSPCA, *1906 Annual Report* (London, 1906), p. 127.

39 Anon., 'Demonstrations at a Meet of the Bucks Otter Hounds',
    Cruel Sports (June 1931), p. 51. The incident was also reported in
    local newspapers such as the *Oxford Times.*

40 The HSA first used their scent-dulling compound, 'Chemical X',
    against the Culmstock OH in April 1964.

41 According to the HSA (2009), when nine saboteurs visited the
    Culmstock OH on 2 May 1965, their 'vehicles were surrounded,
    windows smashed and the occupants assaulted with otter poles
    and whips.' The subsequent scuffle left Leo Lewis, the sabs driver,
    badly beaten with a broken jaw. At www.hsa.enviroweb.org.

42 Ibid., p. 3.

43 On occasions deer-hunters hunted and killed hinds in calf.

44 'Otter-Hunting', *Cruel Sports* (August 1939), p. 58.

45 Bertram Lloyd, *A Vile Sport: Facts About Otterhunting* (Harpenden,
    1945), p. 8.

46 Herbert Ernest Bates, *Otters and Men* (London, 1938), p. 1.

47 Lloyd, *A Vile Sport*, p. 9.

48 Joseph Collinson, *The Hunted Otter* (London, 1911), p. 20. A small part of this pamphlet, which included this quote, was reprinted in *Cruel Sports* magazine in 1929. Covering two pages, it was re-titled '"Sport" and the Otter'.

49 William Lisle Blenkinsopp Coulson, 'The Otter Worry', in *British Blood Sports: 'Let us Go Out and Kill Something'*, ed. Henry S. Salt (London, 1901), p. 36.

50 William Lisle Blenkinsopp Coulson, 'Otter Worrying – A Protest', *The Humanitarian* (August 1908), pp. 60–61.

51 Lloyd, *A Vile Sport*, p. 1.

5 THE LITERARY OTTER

1 Otters are briefly mentioned in Charles Kingsley's *The Water-Babies, A Fairy Tale for a Land Baby* (London, 1863). Beatrix Potter refers to 'wicked otters' in *The Tale of Mr Tod* (London, 1912). Saki's (Hector Hugh Munro) anthology *Beasts and Super-Beasts* (London, 1914) features a short story called 'Laura'. In this the title character dies and is reincarnated as a destructive otter.

2 Kenneth Grahame, *The Wind in The Willows* (Hemel Hempstead, 1992), p. 22.

3 Ibid., p. 22.

4 Ibid., p. 16.

5 Ibid., pp. 65–6.

6 Thornton W. Burgess Society, at www.thorntonburgess.org.

7 *Little Joe Otter* was first published in England in 1935.

8 Thornton W. Burgess, *Little Joe Otter* (London, 1935), p. 9.

9 Ibid., pp. 1–2.

10 Ibid., p. 24.

11 Ibid., p. 9.

12 Ibid., p. 32.

13 Ibid., p. 69.

14 Ibid., p. 71.

15 Ibid., p. 99.

16 Henry Williamson, *Tarka the Otter* (London, 1995), p. 6.

17 Ibid., pp. 265–7.

18 Henry Williamson, 'Letter to T. E. Lawrence', 8 March 1928, cited in Anne Williamson, *Henry Williamson: Tarka and the Last Romantic* (Frome, 1997) p. 96; J. C. Tregarthen, *The Life Story of an Otter* (London, 1909).

19 This annual prize for 'work of imaginative literature' was first instituted in 1919. It considered all novels by British authors under forty-one years of age.

20 'The Hawthornden Prize: Presentation to Mr Henry Williamson', *The Times*, 13 June 1928, p. 11.

21 Cited in Anne Williamson, ed., 'Some Leaves from HW's Own Scrapbook', *The Henry Williamson Society Journal: Tarka Diamond Jubilee Issue*, September 1987, p. 31.

22 Charles Watkins, David Matless, and Paul Merchant, 'Chapter Seven: Science, Sport and the Otter, 1945–1978', in *Our Hunting Fathers*, ed. Richard Hoyle (Lancaster, 2007), p. 176.

23 Williamson, 'Editorial', September 1987, p. 2.

24 Ted Hughes, address given at Henry Williamson's funeral in 1977 cited in Williamson, *Henry Williamson*, p. 335.

25 Emil E. Liers, *An Otter's Story* (London, 1954), p. 9.

26 'Animals: Artful Otters', *Time*, 27 February 1939.

27 Cathy Wurzer, *Tales of the Road: Highway 61* (St Paul, MN, 2008), p. 118.

28 Liers, *An Otter's Story* (London, 1954), p. 6.

29 Frances Pitt, *Moses, My Otter* (London, 1927), p. 9.

30 Ibid., p. 35.

31 Ibid., p. 20.

32 Ibid., p. 70

33 Ibid., p. 90.

34 John Scott Henderson, *Report on the Committee on Cruelty to Wild Animals* (London, 1951).

35 Henry Williamson, 'On Otters', in *The Linhay on the Downs* (London, 1934), pp. 187–93, p. 187.

36 Phyllis Kelway, *The Otter Book* (London, 1944), p. 27.

37 Ibid., p. 132.

38 Sadly a fire destroyed the house and took the life of Edal in 1968.

39 Maxwell renamed Sandaig as Camusfèarna (Gaelic for 'The Bay of Alders') to help protect the true location of his home.

40 'Introduction', in Gavin Maxwell, *The Ring of Bright Water Trilogy* (London, 2001), p. xvii.

41 Ibid., p. 78.

42 A children's version of the book, *The Otters' Tale*, was published in 1962. Two further autobiographical novels followed in 1963, *The Rocks Remain*, and 1968, *Raven Seek Thy Brother*.

43 Maxwell, *Ring of Bright Water Trilogy*, p. 7.

44 Gavin Maxwell 'Letter to Raef Payne' [1956], cited in Douglas Botting, *The Saga of Ring of Bright Water: The Enigma of Gavin Maxwell* (Glasgow, 2004), p. 187.

45 Maxwell, *Ring of Bright Water Trilogy*, p. 102.

46 Botting, *Saga of Ring of Bright Water*, p. 197.

47 Maxwell, *Ring of Bright Water Trilogy*, p. 122.

48 Ibid., p. 93.

49 Ibid., p. 100.

50 Ibid., p. 211.

51 Botting, *Saga of Ring of Bright Water*, p. 302.

52 Austin Chinn, 'Introduction' to Maxwell, *Ring of Bright Water Trilogy*, p. xix.

53 Botting, *Saga of Ring of Bright Water*, p. xvi.

54 Walter Von Sanden, *Ingo, My Otter* (1959); Ernest G. Neal, *Topsy & Turvy, My Two Otters* (1961); Elaine Hurrell, *Watch for the Otter* (1963); Morna Eyres, *Otter in our Parlour* (1963); Dorophy Wisbeski *An Otter in the House: the Story of Okee* (1964); J. A. Davis, *Beever and Company* (1969); Philip Wayre, *The River People* (1976); Marna Fyson, *Stinkerbelle, the Nark* (1976); Daphne Neville, *Bee, a Particular Otter* 1982); Rex Harper, *An Otter on the Aga: And Other True Tales from an Animal Sanctuary* (2007).

55 Mortimer Batten, *The Wandering Otter* (1947); Rhoda Leonard and William S. Briscoe, *Sleeky the Otter* (1964); J. A. Davis, *Samaki, the Story of an Otter in Africa* (1979); Ian Saint-Barbe Anderson,

A Tangle of Otters (1984); Ian Saint-Barbe Anderson, *A Travelling Otter* (1985); David Chaffe, *Stormforce* (1999); Bridget MacCaskill, *A Private Sort of Life* (2002).

56 Joe Barber-Starkey, *Jason and the Sea Otter* (1997); Lucy Daniels, *Otter in the Outhouse* (1998); Barbara Helen Berger, *A Lot of Otters* (2000); Jill Tomlinson, *The Otter Who Wanted to Know* (2004); Adrienne Kennaway, *Otter's First Swim* (2005); Lisa, Adam and Zachery Hartley, *The Adventures of Otto the Otter* (2005); Crystal Bowman, *Otter and Owl Say I'm Sorry* (2008); Tudor Humphries, *Otter Moon* (2009); Nora Dohlke, *Wonderful Adventures of Ozzie the Sea Otter* (2009).

6 THE OTTER ON SCREEN

1 Anne Williamson, *Henry Williamson: Tarka and the Last Romantic* (Frome, 1997), p. 281.

2 Season 7, Episode 26.

3 Montgomery also adapted the script into a new book for Disney. *The Odyssey Of An Otter: A Fact-Fiction Nature Story* was published in 1960.

4 Reintroduction schemes became increasingly popular among wildlife management agencies. According to the IUCN (2008) over 4,000 river otters have been reintroduced in the United States since 1976.

5 Rutherford Montgomery, *The Living Wilderness* (Caldwell, ID, 2001), p. 31.

6 Ibid., p. 34.

7 Douglas Botting, *The Saga of Ring of Bright Water: The Enigma of Gavin Maxwell* (Glasgow, 2004), p. 485.

8 Ibid., p. 529.

9 Virginia McKenna, *The Life in My Years* (London, 2009), pp. 86–7.

10 Virginia McKenna recalls filming Ring of Bright Water in 1968', *Telegraph Magazine*, 28 March 2009, p. 82.

11 Ibid., p. 82.

12 Botting, *Saga of Ring of Bright Water*, p. 529.

13 McKenna, *Life in My Years*, pp. 90–91.

14 Botting, *Saga of Ring of Bright Water*, p. 486.

15 Henry Williamson, diary extract, 27 June 1971, cited in Anne Williamson, *Henry Williamson: Tarka and the Last Romantic* (Frome, 1997), p. 317.

16 David Cobham, 'The Making of the Film Tarka,' in *The Henry Williamson Society Journal, Tarka Diamond Jubilee Issue*, ed. Anne Williamson, September 1987, p. 25.

17 Ibid., p. 25.

18 Ibid., p. 27.

19 Williamson, *Henry Williamson*, p. 333.

20 John Goldsmith, *Tarkina the Otter* (London, 1981), p. 17.

21 Ibid., p. 20.

22 Ibid., p. 22.

23 Ibid., p. 23.

24 John J. O'Connor, *New York Times*, 15 December 1980.

25 Surprisingly, the otter has remained largely unseen in animated productions. *Canadian Sesame Street* introduced Louis the Otter to the series in the 1980s. This new Muppet character was a French-speaking sea otter. In the United States Disney aired the cartoon series *PB&J Otter* from 1998 to 2000. In Britain a little-known stop-motion animation series called *Doctor Otter* was shown on BBC 2 in 2001 and 2002.

26 The otter has featured in several of BBC's pioneering wildlife series: *The Living Planet* (1984), *World of Wildlife* (2001), *Life of Mammals* (2003) and *Planet Earth* (2006). All are narrated by Sir David Attenborough. More recently Philippa Forrester and Charlie Hamilton James have made three excellent programmes about the animal: *An Otter in the Family* (2007), *Saving Grace the Otter* (2008) and *Natural World: On the Trail of Tarka* (2008). In Spring 2010 BBC1 also aired *Halcyon River Diaries*. This fascinating four-part series records life on a typical English river through the eyes of Charlie, Philippa and their three young sons. Mayfly, moorhens, kingfishers and otters are just a few of their wild neighbours.

27 Transcript of J. K. Rowling's live interview on www.scholastic.com, 16 October 2000.

7 PROTECTING THE OTTER

1 Although national laws and international treaties do exist, they are ignored in certain parts of the world. A common difficulty with conservation is convincing people that wildlife has an intrinsic value. Also, some countries – such as Indonesia – have signed up to CITES, preventing international trade, but have no internal laws protecting otters.
2 Hans Kruuk, *Otters: Ecology, Behaviour, and Conservation* (Oxford, 2006), p. 28.
3 Pat Foster-Turley, 'Conservation Aspects of the Ecology of Asian Small-clawed and Smooth Otters on the Malay Peninsula', *IUCN Otter Specialist Group Bulletin*, 7 (1992), p. 29, cited in Kruuk, *Otters*, p. 227.
4 Ian Chillcott cited by Jasper Copping and Graham Mole, 'Anglers Call for Cull of Otters over Fish Havoc', *Telegraph*, 7 June 2009.
5 Ibid.
6 S. K. Eltringham, *Wildlife Resources and Economic Development* (Chichester, 1984), cited in Kruuk, *Otters*, p. 229.
7 R. Alvarez and G. Medina-Vogel, 'Lontra Felina', in *IUCN Red List of Threatened Species*, at www.iucnredlist.org, (2008).
8 IOSF, *The Alarming Trade in Otter Furs* (Isle of Skye, 2008).
9 'Otter: Dressed to Kill', *Times of India News Network*, September 2005, cited in ibid.
10 Paul Yoxon, 'International Campaign Against Fur Trade Launched to Protect Otters', www.wildlifeextras.com, 17 April 2007.
11 Paul Yoxon cited in IOSF, 'Dara the Otter is Star of the East!', online press release at www.otter.org, 17 December 2008.
12 Kruuk, *Otters*, p. 225.
13 Nicole Duplaix, *Giant Otter Final Report: Guianas Rapid River Bio-assessments and Giant Otter Conservation Project*, www.giantotterresearch.com/articles/WWF_Giant_otter_Report_PDF

Mini.pdf (2002), p. 117.

14 James A. Estes, 'Catastrophes and Conservation: Lessons from Sea Otters and the Exxon Valdez', *Science*, CCLIV/5038 (13 December 1991), p. 1596.

15 The California Department of Fish and Game has a marine mammal care facility with an excellent treatment programme for oiled otters. In 2009 an oiled sea otter, named Olive, was successfully released after six weeks of rehabilitation. A tracking device was implanted to monitor her health in the wild.

16 C. Kreuder et al., 'Patterns of Mortality in Southern Sea Otters (Enhydra lutris nereis) from 1998–2001', *Journal of Wildlife Diseases*, XXXIX/3 (2003), pp. 495–509.

17 Kruuk, *Otters*, p. 208.

18 Paul Chanin, *The Natural History of Otters* (London, 1985), p. 134.

19 Charles Watkins, David Matless and Paul Merchant, 'Science, Sport and the Otter, 1945–1978', in *Our Hunting Fathers: Field Sports in England after 1850*, ed. Richard Hoyle (Lancaster, 2007), p. 170.

20 *Report of the Committee on Cruelty to Wild Animals* (London, 1951), p. 77.

21 Ibid., p. 82.

22 Marie Stephens, *The Otter Report* (London, 1957), p. 8.

23 Max Nicholson, 'Nicholson to Hume,' 17 March 1958, cited in Watkins et al., 'Science, Sport and the Otter, 1945–1978', p. 175.

24 Jack Ivestor Lloyd, 'Where are the Otters?' *Gamekeeper and Countryside*, August 1962, p. 299.

25 Ibid., p. 300.

26 Mammal Society, 'The Otter in Britain,' *Oryx*, 10 (1969), pp. 16–22, pp. 16, 20

27 Ibid., p. 16.

28 Hansard (Commons Parliamentary Debates), Protection of Otters Bill, 13 May 1969, p. 1223.

29 Ibid., p. 1223.

30 Hansard (Commons Parliamentary Debates), Protection of Otters Bill, 29 February 1972, p. 256.

31 Ibid., p. 257.

32 'Philip Reflects on a Life with Animals', *Beccles and Bungay Journal*, 29 March 2007.

33 Philip Wayre, *Operation Otter* (London, 1989), p. 57.

34 Mammal Society, 'The Otter in Britain – a Second Report', *Oryx*, 12 (1974), pp. 429–35, p. 429.

35 R. H. West, 'The Suffolk Otter Survey', *Suffolk Natural History*, 16 (1975), pp. 378–88; S. Macdonald and C. F. Mason, 'The Status of the Otter (*Lutra lutra L.*) in Norfolk', *Biological Conservation*, 19 (1976), pp. 119–24.

36 Although a recommendation of legal protection was made, the elusive nature of the animal meant its status could not be agreed. From the limited evidence available the species was not rare enough to be endangered, and therefore could not be protected under the Conservation of Wild Creatures and Plants Act 1975. For this to change, proof of an imminent extinction had to be proven.

37 Although scientists did not blame the sport for the animal's predicament, its role was not overlooked. Killing continued after the onset of the decline. From 1958 to 1963 a total of 1065 otters were killed by active hunts.

38 Paul Chanin and Don Jefferies, 'The Decline of the Otter *Lutra lutra L.* in Britain: An Analysis of Hunting Records and Discussion of Causes', *Biological Journal of the Linnean Society*, 10 (1978), pp. 305–28, p. 325.

39 Philip Wayre, *Operation Otter* (London, 1989), p. 154.

40 Joint Nature Conservation Committee, *Second Report by the United Kingdom under Article 17 on the implementation of the Habitats Directive from January 2001 to December 2006* (Peterborough, 2007).

41 Robin Page, 'The Man who Saved Britain's Otters: One Man's Crusade to Save Britain's Otters', *The Telegraph*, 5 February 2009

42 Fran Southgate, of Sussex Wildlife Trust, cited by John Ingham, '40 Years after Vanishing, Otters Return Nationwide', *Sunday Express*, 22 July 2009.

Select Bibliography

Adair, Rod, *A Chain of Bubbles* (Powys, 1999)
—, *Reflections Along a Chain* (Powys, 2001)
Allan, Alexander, *Hunting the Sea Otter* (London, 1910)
Allen, Daniel, 'The Cultural and Historical Geographies of Otter
    Hunting in Britain, 1830–1939', PhD thesis, University of
    Nottingham (2006)
—, '"A Delightful Sport with Peculiar Claims": The Specificities of
    Otter Hunting, 1850–1939', in *Our Hunting Fathers: Field Sports in
    England after 1850*, ed. Richard Hoyle (Lancaster, 2007), pp. 143–64
Barker, Kathleen Frances, *The Young Entry: Fox-Hunting, Beagling and
    Otter-hunting for Beginners* (London, 1939)
Batchelor, Rev. John, *The Ainu and Their Folklore* (London, 1901)
Bates, Herbert Ernest, *Otters and Men* (London, 1938)
Bell-Irving, David Jardine, *Tally-Ho: Fifty Years of Sporting
    Reminiscences* (Dumfries, 1920)
Bininda-Emonds, Olaf R. P., John L. Gittleman and Andy Purvis,
    'Building Large Trees by Combining Phylogenetic Information:
    A Complete Phylogeny of the Extant Carnivora (Mammalia)',
    Biological Reviews, 74 (1999), pp. 143–75
Bingley, William, *Animal Biography, or, Popular Zoology* (London,
    1829)
Black, Lydia, *Russians in Alaska, 1732–1867* (Fairbanks, AL, 2004)
Blaine, Delabere Pritchett, ed., *An Encyclopaedia of Rural Sports*
    (London, 1840)
Bonner, Gerald, David Rollason and Clare Stancliffe, *St Cuthbert, his*

Cult and his Community to AD 1200 (Woodbridge, 1998)

Botting, Douglas, *The Saga of Ring of Bright Water: The Enigma of Gavin Maxwell* (Glasgow, 2004)

Burgess, Thornton W., *Little Joe Otter* (London, 1935)

Cameron, Ludovic Charles Richard, *Otters and Otter-Hunting* (London, 1908)

—, *Otter Hunting* (London, 1938)

Chanin, Paul, *The Natural History of Otters* (London, 1985)

—, and Don Jefferies, 'The Decline of the Otter *Lutra lutra L.* in Britain: An Analysis of Hunting Records and Discussion of Causes', *Biological Journal of the Linnean Society*, 10 (1978), pp. 305–28

Cheesman, Walter, and Mildred Cheesman, *Diaries of the Crowhurst Otter Hounds* (n.p., 1904)

Clapham, Richard, *The Book of the Otter* (London, 1922)

Cobham, David, 'The Making of the Film Tarka', in *The Henry Williamson Society Journal, Tarka Diamond Jubilee Issue,* ed. Anne Williamson, September 1987

Collinson, Joseph, *The Hunted Otter* (London, 1911)

Coulson, William Lisle Blenkinsopp, 'The Otter Worry', in *British Blood Sports: 'Let Us Go Out and Kill Something'*, ed. Henry S. Salt (London, 1901)

—, 'Otter Worrying – A Protest', *The Humanitarian* (August 1908), pp. 60–61

Davis, Joseph A., *Samaki, the Story of an Otter in Africa* (London, 1979)

Duplaix, Nicole, 'Observations on the Ecology and Behavior of the Giant River Otter *Pteronura brasiliensis* in Suriname', *Revue d'Ecologie (Terre Vie)*, 34 (1980), pp. 495–620

—, *Giant Otter Final Report: Guiana's Rapid River Bio-assessments and Giant Otter Conservation Project*, www.giantotterresearch.com/articles/wwf_Giant_otter_Report_pdfMini.pdf (2002)

Elliott, Henry W., *Our Arctic Province* (New York, 1886)

Etter, Carl, *Ainu Folklore: Traditions and Culture of the Vanishing Aborigines of Japan, 1949* (New York, 2004)

Foster-Turley, Pat, 'Conservation Aspects of the Ecology of Asian Small-clawed and Smooth Otters on the Malay Peninsula', *IUCN*

Otter Specialist Group Bulletin, 7 (1992), pp. 26–9

—, Sheila Macdonald and Chris Mason, *Otters: An Action Plan for their Conservation*, IUCN (1990)

Fuller, Max F., *Sacred Books of the East* (Oxford, 1879)

Gelert, Fore, *Fore Gelert's Guide to the Foxhounds and Staghounds of England; to which are added, the Otter-Hounds and Harriers of several counties* (London, 1849)

Gibson, James R., *Otter Skins, Boston Ships, and China Goods: The Maritime Fur Trade of the Northwest Coast, 1785–1841* (London, 1999)

Goldsmith, John, *Tarkina the Otter* (London, 1981)

Grahame, Kenneth, *The Wind in The Willows* [1908] (Hemel Hempstead, 1992)

Hansard (Commons Parliamentary Debates), *Protection of Otters Bill*, 13 May 1969, pp. 1222–7

—, *Protection of Otters Bill*, 29 February 1972, pp. 255–8

Howes, Colin Antony, 'The Decline of the Otter in South Yorkshire and Adjacent Areas', *Naturalist*, 101 (1976), pp. 3–12

Hurrell, Elaine, *Watch for the Otter* (London, 1963)

Ingham, John, '40 Years after Vanishing, Otters Return Nationwide', *Sunday Express*, 22 July 2009

IOSF, *The Alarming Trade in Otter Furs* (Isle of Skye, 2008)

—, 'Dara the Otter is Star of the East!' online press release, 17 December 2008

Ivester Lloyd, Jack, *Come Hunting!* (London, 1952)

—, 'Where are the Otters?' *Gamekeeper and Countryside* (August 1962), p. 299

Kelway, Phyllis, *The Otter Book* (London, 1944)

Koepfli, Klaus-Peter, and Robert K. Wayne, 'Phylogenetic Relationships of Otter (Carnivora: Mustelidae) Based on Mitochondrial Cytochrome B Sequences', *Journal of Zoology*, 246 (1998), pp. 401–16

Joint Nature Conservation Committee, *Second Report by the UK under Article 17 on the implementation of the Habitats Directive from January 2001 to December 2006* (Peterborough, 2007)

King, Angela, John Ottaway and Angela Potter, *The Declining Otter: A Guide to its Conservation* (Chaffcombe, 1976)

Kreuder, C., et al., 'Patterns of Mortality in Southern Sea Otters (Enhydra lutris nereis) from 1998–2001', *Journal of Wildlife Diseases*, XXXIX/3 (2003), pp. 495–509

Kruuk, Hans, *Otters: Ecology, Behaviour and Conservation* (Oxford, 2006)

—, 'Otters (*Lutra lutra*) in Swedish Prehistory – with Notes on Behaviour', *IUCN Otter Specialist Group Bulletin*, XXV/1 (2008), pp. 28–31

Laidler, Keith, and Liz Laidler, *The River Wolf* (London, 1983)

Liers, Emil E., *An Otter's Story* (London, 1954)

Littlepage, Dean, *Steller's Island: Adventures of a Pioneer Naturalist in Alaska* (Seattle, WA, 2006)

Lloyd, Bertram, *A Vile Sport. Facts About Otterhunting* (Harpenden, 1945)

Lomax, James, *Diary of Otter Hunting* (Liverpool, 1892)

Love, John A., *Sea Otters* (London, 1990)

Macdonald Hastings, Douglas, 'Hunting the Otter', *Picture Post* (22 July 1939), pp. 52–6

Macdonald, S., and C. F. Mason, 'The Status of the Otter (*Lutra lutra* L.) in Norfolk', *Biological Conservation*, 19 (1976), pp. 119–24

Mammal Society, 'The Otter in Britain', *Oryx*, 10 (1969), pp. 16–22

—, 'The Otter in Britain – a Second Report', *Oryx*, 12 (1974), pp. 429–35

Mason, C. F., and S. Macdonald, *Otters: Ecology and Conservation* (Cambridge, 1986)

Matless, David, Paul Merchant and Charles Watkins, 'Animal Landscapes: Otters and Wildfowl in England 1945–1970', *Transactions of the Institute of British Geographers*, 30 (2005), pp. 191–205

Maxwell, Gavin, *The Otters' Tale* (London, 1962)

—, *The Rocks Remain* (London, 1963)

—, *Raven Seek Thy Brother* (London, 1968)

—, *The Ring of Bright Water Trilogy* (London, 2001)

McCracken, Harold, *Hunters of the Stormy Sea* (London, 1957)

McKenna, Virginia, *The Life in My Years* (London, 2009)

—, 'Virginia McKenna Recalls Filming *Ring of Bright Water* in 1968', *Telegraph Magazine*, 28 March 2009, p. 82

Montgomery, Rutherford, *The Odyssey Of An Otter: A Fact-Fiction Nature Story* (New York, 1960).

—, *The Living Wilderness* (Caldwell, ID, 2001)

Mott, Geoffrey R., *Records of the Dartmoor Otter Hounds, 1740–1940* (Dartmoor, 1970)

Nickerson, Roy, *Sea Otters: A Natural History and Guide* (San Francisco, 1989)

Paine, Stephani, *The Nature of Sea Otters: A Story of Survival* (Vancouver, 1993)

Pitt, Frances, *Moses, My Otter* (London, 1927)

Pring, Geoffrey, *Records of the Culmstock Otterhounds, c. 1790–1957* (Exeter, 1958)

RSPCA, *1906 Annual Report* (London, 1906)

Scammon, Charles Melville, *The Marine Mammalia of the Northwestern Coast of America* (New York, 1874)

Scott Henderson, John, *Report on the Committee on Cruelty to Wild Animals* (London, 1951)

Turnbull, William, *Recollections of an Otter Hunter* (Farrow-on-Tyne, 1896)

Skeat, Walter, and F. H. Townsend, *Fables and Folk Tales from an Eastern Forest* (Cambridge, 1901)

Stephens, Marie, *The Otter Report* (London, 1957)

Tregarthen, John Coulson, *The Life Story of an Otter* (London, 1909)

Walsh, John Henry, *British Rural Sports* (London, 1856)

Walton, Isaak, *The Complete Angler: Or Contemplative Man's Recreation* (London, 1896)

Watkins, Charles, David Matless and Paul Merchant, 'Science, Sport and the Otter, 1945–1978', in *Our Hunting Fathers: Field Sports in England after 1850*, ed. Richard Hoyle (Lancaster, 2007)

Wayre, Philip, *The River People* (Glasgow, 1977)

—, *Operation Otter* (London, 1989)

—, 'Philip Reflects on a Life with Animals', *Beccles and Bungay Journal*, 29 March 2007

West, R. H., 'The Suffolk Otter Survey', *Suffolk Natural History* (1975), pp. 378–88

White, Gilbert, *The Natural History and Antiquities of Selborne* (London, 1837)

Williamson, Anne, ed, *The Henry Williamson Society Journal: Tarka Diamond Jubilee Issue,* September 1987

—, *Henry Williamson: Tarka and the Last Romantic* (Frome, 1997)

Williamson, Henry, *Tarka the Otter* [1927] (London, 1995)

—, *The Linhay on the Downs* (London, 1934)

Yoxon, Paul, 'International Campaign Against Fur Trade Launched to Protect Otters', www.wildlifeextras.com, 17 April 2007

Websites and Associations

AMBLONYX OTTER SITE
www.amblonyx.com

BEENIE'S WORLD OF OTTERS
www.sophieneville.co.uk/BEENIE/index.html

DEFENDERS OF WILDLIFE
www.defenders.org

DEPARTMENT OF FISH AND GAME, CALIFORNIA
www.dfg.ca.gov

FRIENDS OF THE SEA OTTER
www.seaotters.org

FURGET-ME-NOT
www.furgetmenot.org.uk

GIANT OTTER RESEARCH
www.giantotterresearch.com

THE HENRY WILLIAMSON SOCIETY
www.henrywilliamson.co.uk

INTERNATIONAL OTTER SURVIVAL FUND (IOSF)
www.otter.org

INTERNATIONAL UNION FOR CONSERVATION OF NATURE
www.iucn.org

IUCN RED LIST OF THREATENED SPECIES
www.iucnredlist.org/

IUCN OTTER SPECIALIST GROUP
www.otterspecialistgroup.org

LEAGUE AGAINST CRUEL SPORTS
www.league.org.uk

NEPAL OTTER PROJECT
www.ottersnepal.org

OTTER JOY
www.otterjoy.com

THE RIVER OTTER ALLIANCE
www.otternet.com/ROA/index.htm

SEA OTTER ALLIANCE
www.seaotterresearch.org

WORLD ASSOCIATION OF ZOOS AND AQUARIUMS
www.waza.org

Acknowledgements

The IUCN Otter Specialist Group has been producing research and promoting otter conservation since 1974. The dedication and knowledge of its members, past and present, has been an inspiration. I would like to personally thank Lesley Wright, Hans Kruuk, Nicole Duplaix, Jan Reed-Smith, Grace Yoxon and Paul Yoxon for their assistance and encouragement.

Thanks to Jonathan Burt, series editor, and Michael Leaman, publisher, for welcoming *Otter* to the Animal series. Their comments and support were much appreciated. I am also grateful to the Reaktion team for their help.

I appreciate the generosity of Mike Huskisson, and useful correspondence with Anne Williamson, David Cobham, Virginia McKenna, Philip Wayre and Rod Adair.

The Arts and Humanities Research Council funded my doctoral research on otter hunting, at the University of Nottingham (Award No. 02/63215). Thanks to both for their support, also to Charles Watkins and David Matless for their excellent advice.

Finally, special thanks must go to my parents, Tim and Janice, and brother Chris for their kindness and ongoing support. I am also indebted to Anna McLaren for her encouragement, advice and good company. Without you this book would not have been possible.

Photo Acknowledgements

The author and publishers wish to express their thanks to the below sources of illustrative material and/or permission to reproduce it:

Dmitry Azovtsev: p. 14 bottom; Courtesy of *Country Life*: pp. 11 right, 101, 112; Mike Baird, flickr.bairdphotos.com: pp. 25 centre left, 60, 139; Bodleian Library: p. 37; Department of Fish and Game, California: p. 138; Disney Enterprises, INC: p. 128; Nicole Duplaix: pp. 17 top, 18, 19, 136; Friends of the Sea Otter, www.seaotter.org: p. 25 centre right; Frick Art: p. 64; By Aidan Hart, www.aidanharticons.com; p. 29: Courtesy of Michael Huskisson, ACIG: pp. 78, 84, 86, 87, 89, 145; IOSF: pp. 21, 134, 135 bottom; ITV Studios Global Entertainment: pp. 123, 124, 126, 127; Matt Knoth: p. 25 top right; Hans Kruuck, 2008: p. 30; Bernard Landgraf: p. 146; Andrea McLaren: p. 24; Neil McIntosh: p. 22 bottom; Gavin Maxwell Enterprises Ltd: pp. 108, 110, 111; David Monniaux: p. 17 bottom; NOAA Historic Fisheries Collection: pp. 56 (Stefan Claesson), 57 (Stefan Claesson); NOAA Library Collection: p. 54 (Mr Sean Linehan, NOS, NGS); NOAA National Marine Fisheries Service: p. 52; Dave Pape: p. 6; Elfyn Pugh: p. 135 top right; Rex Features: pp. 118 (Everett Collection), 120 (Everett Collection); Sage Ross: p. 13 bottom; Reproduced by permission of the Estate of C. F. Tunnicliffe RA, OBE: p. 97; Historic Collections, University of Aberdeen: p. 28; University of California: pp. 34, 35; US Fish and Wildlife Services, National Digital Library: p. 137; US National Library of Medicine: pp. 41, 45; Shaun Williams: p. 43; Mila Zinkova: p. 49; Zoological Society of London: pp. 9, 10, 44.

Index